A
HANDBOOK
TO
MARRIAGE

Theodor Bovet

DOLPHIN BOOKS
DOUBLEDAY & COMPANY, INC.
GARDEN CITY, NEW YORK

FOREWORD

Just twenty years ago a group of professional people in the United States met together and established a new organization, designed to foster the study of marriage and family relationships and to develop on the basis of that study new services to the community. This organization became in time the National Council on Family Relations, out of which later emerged the American Association of Marriage Counselors.

In that same year, 1938, a similar group of professional people met in England and established an organization with virtually the same objectives. It became in time the National Marriage Guidance Council.

With the passing of the years these two organizations became aware of each other's existence, and a fruitful exchange of ideas and experiences took place. Out of this and other similar sharing of ideas has come a new movement in the English-speaking world. Through study and research, education and clinical experience, we have come in these past twenty years to a greatly increased understanding of the marriage relationship.

While this was happening, a new awareness of the need to study marriage was also dawning in continental Europe. No movement of equivalent dimensions took shape there, however. Progress was therefore slower and was confined largely to the creative thinking of a few individual pioneers —both Catholic and Protestant. Barriers of language isolated these thinkers from the fruitful interchange that was going on in the English-speaking world.

Conspicuous among these continental students of marriage was Theodor Bovet. He was not a detached theorist. A Swiss physician with a wide comprehension of the significance of modern psychology, he found a rich laboratory in his clinical experience of dealing with the marital problems which, as his fame increased, were brought to him in increasing numbers. While he studied and observed his patients, he searched the available literature for deeper understanding of their needs. He did not confine himself to scientific knowledge. A man of deep religious faith, he sought to bring the insights of theology and philosophy also to bear upon the task to which he had dedicated himself.

In 1952 the International Union of Family Organizations, a consultative body of the UN and UNESCO, with its headquarters in Paris, decided to set up an International Commission on Marriage Guidance and asked me to become its chairman. Thus for the first time the stream of thinking in the English-speaking world was brought into touch, in the form of a series of sustained personal encounters, with the comparatively isolated little band of continental European pioneers.

It became clear at once that, in Protestant circles at least, one man stood out among the others. This man was Theodor Bovet. His skill as a marriage counselor was widely known throughout his own country. As a lecturer he had traveled farther afield—I recently encountered quite casually, in Upper Thailand, a German who remembered with gratitude an address given by him to the students of Tübingen University. His books, written both in French and German, enjoyed an even wider circulation.

Those of us who have had the privilege of meeting this wise, kind, and humble man have been refreshed by his depth of thought and experience. He speaks little English, however; so until now many who might have been stimulated and challenged by his philosophy have not had the opportunity to take the measure of his mind. The publication of this excellent translation of one of his best books brings this unhappy state of affairs to an end—a fact concerning which I greatly rejoice.

I count it a high privilege to have been asked to introduce this readable yet profound little volume to American readers. It is simply enough written to be entirely readable by those who make no claim to being students of the subject but who seek help in making their own married lives richer and more rewarding. Such readers will find a wealth of stimulating and challenging new ideas. I cannot believe that there exists a married man or woman who will not be the better for reading what Dr. Bovet, out of his lifelong experience, has to say.

The value of the book does not, however, end there. Behind the easy, effortless style with which Dr. Bovet writes there is a wealth of tried and tested wisdom which is the fruit of deep reflection. I believe that no serious student of marriage, no teacher or counselor in the family field can afford to ignore the contribution Dr. Bovet has to make to our quest for a wholesome, balanced understanding of the true nature of the relationship between man and woman. The extraordinary breadth of this thought, combining as it does the approaches of medicine, of psychology, of philosophy, and of theology, entitles him to be heard with attention and respect.

Those who are familiar with the current American lit-

erature in this field will at once find in Dr. Bovet a fresh-
ness of approach, a penetrating depth of insight and inter-
pretation, which will delight and challenge them. It has
been a long time since I read a book on marriage in which
I have so frequently been impelled to reach for my pencil
to mark and underline a passage for further thought and
reflection.

Dr. Bovet not only delights us, however. Again and
again he challenges our materialistic, pleasure-toned way of
life, our lack of spiritual depth, our insensitivity. As we
measure our lives together as husbands and wives against
the goals to which the book points us, we shall be humbled
and chastened.

To me the supreme quality of Dr. Bovet's message is
that he opens up for us, as very few writers can, what I
have sometimes called "the higher reaches" of the shared
life which become possible to men and women in marriage,
and that in doing so he exposes ruthlessly the false dichot-
omy of sex and love on the one hand and religious experience and aspiration on the other, which has so long
cast a dark shadow upon our Western culture. Dr. Bovet
has a specialist's understanding of the new scientific approach to sex and marriage. But he has something more
that gives to his thinking a vaster dimension—the realization that all our struggles to comprehend the meaning of
human life and human love are doomed to futility unless
they recognize the relevance of a spiritual and eternal
perspective.

DAVID R. MACE

CONTENTS

INTRODUCTION

For the New Edition

Today for most people the man-woman relationship is decisive. It can lead to the discovery of self, neighbor, and God, or it can lead to hopeless entanglement and inner ruin. This is as true of the unmarried as it is of the married, and the answer is the same in both cases: it is that love should govern the whole field of sexuality, and that God should govern the whole field of love.

This is the thesis to be presented in this book. I shall try to throw some light on the problem of marriage, while not forgetting the concrete details of everyday life. I shall speak clearly and soberly and call things by their real names, so that the ordinary man and woman can understand what I am getting at. But I shall never forget the one basic fact that lies behind all marriage. Behind the tangible relationship between any man and any woman stands a great mystery—and not somewhere on the edge of it, but involved in even the slightest action within it.

Only against such a background can we understand the visible and concrete fact of marriage; without this background we must inevitably go on misunderstanding marriage.

In 1955 this book took the place of an earlier publication, *Die Ehe, ihre Krise und Neuwerdung*. In the meantime, that version, too, has been repeatedly corrected, emended and updated to include all the latest knowledge regarding marriage relationships. The whole discipline of marriage study is still young and therefore subject to revision of opinions, especially, I feel, as the Protestant and Roman Catholic views regarding marriage no longer seem as irreconcilable as they used to be. In fact, I would like to say, we can now speak of a unified Christian view of marriage with only minor diversions regarding detail. Both Catholic and Protestant approaches have changed and, to be honest, we, the Protestants, must acknowledge that we have certainly profited from the study of insights held by our Catholic brethren. For that matter, we are all still learning.

Marriage is learning too—not only in the sense of becoming a better thing, but above all in the realization that it is not in itself a goal or ultimate aim. It is one of the forms of our transitory and imperfect human life—and at the same time an allegory of that Love which was in the beginning, is today, and always will be.

It is this love of God that gives marriage its contemporary importance. What matters in this day and age is not only the possibilities of making an individual marriage happier—as important as that is; it is not merely a matter of clearing a way through the sexual chaos of this age. What really matters is for us to perceive the message that God reveals to us through the institution of marriage. In an age of political and ideological controversy when even the Gospel is ignored by so many, God speaks to us through the divine bond of marriage. If in marriage we can experience the fullness of His love, we may also be enabled to recreate our relationship to Him and to our neighbor. Thus, today marriage becomes the arena in which we must fight our decisive struggle.

Easter 1968

1.

LOVE AND MARRIAGE

Imagine three different couples. The first are two young people who have just fallen in love; they know practically nothing about each other, but each regards the other as the best and most beautiful person in the world, and they are honestly convinced that no young man and woman have ever before been as completely in love as they are. The second couple are in the mid-forties; all their illusions are over, and they look at each other in the pitiless light of day. The more violently they once desired each other, the more fundamental is their mutual antipathy now. Every word from the wife gets on the husband's nerves, while she responds with a weary ironical smile to what little he has to say—usually about his job. For the sake of the children they keep up outward appearances, but they each have their own personal interests, their own personal "living-space." In this way there is no chance of their being jealous; they are showing what is called commonsense and self-respect. The third couple are also half way between forty and fifty, and they too have outlived their illusions, but they have learned in the process to love each other as they actually are. In fact each has been so absorbed into the other's being that each understands the other's destiny better than he does his own, and they help each other in achieving it. This has not been easy; but now they love each other's personality, even when it conflicts with their own: they support each other unconditionally against the rest of the world, and even against any temptation on the part of the other not to be true to his own self. However hard it may still be at times, they really do belong to each other.

The problem facing every young married couple is how to make sure of developing in the direction of the third pair and not the second. This will not take place as a matter of course; it needs determined effort, and while this has its joys it often also means renunciation. The task of marriage counseling is to assist the young couple in their struggle, showing them what issues have to be faced and what must be allowed just to take its course.

Many attempts have been made to make marriage a happier state. Efforts have been made to secure improvements in the economic position of the family, reforms have been made in the legal status of married persons, comparative studies have been made of male and female psychology; above all, research has been made into every detail of sexual behavior, with the aim of supplying practical directions as to how to attain perfect harmony in this matter. All these things are useful; but the great danger lies in coming to believe that married happiness can be achieved by success in some mere fraction of the whole, and that success can be guaranteed if one confines oneself to this. It reminds one of the attempts that have been made to secure the happiness of mankind by means of vitamins or social security measures. It comes from a failure to realize three things. First, marriage is not a merely economic, a purely psychological, or an exclusively sexual relationship; it is a total association lasting for life—embracing and profoundly altering whole areas of human activity. Therefore, it does not simply involve one man and one woman; it is a living branch of the whole great tree of human society. The relationship between husband and wife helps to determine their place in society at large, and the way they bring up their children has its influence on the future development of that society. Thus, third, marriage does not develop as a matter of course, as a result of impulses and feelings felt by the individual; it demands a continual transformation in him so that his existence may take new forms. Marriage is like a growing organism—an uninterrupted process of change in energy and material, ceaseless alteration of form, never ending revolution. If husband and wife think they have achieved perfection and require no further development, their marriage will quickly die.

These three main aspects of marriage are closely interwoven. Therefore, I shall not deal with them separately, but shall try, working within the classical problems of marriage as these are usually formulated, to trace the connection between them, and so discover new connections and unsuspected solutions. In every case I shall begin by examining the usual basic assumptions and then try to trace their meaning for the whole.

From Bondage to Love

The most primitive human relationship is that between mother and child. The first feeling a mother has for her child is not one of personal love; the child is not yet a personal "Thou" to her, but part of herself. At first, she loves herself in the child—or rather she loves what she would have liked to have been, what she has put into the new creature. The child may be her treasure, or her achievement, or even her god; but not her equal. To the child the mother is home, the ground under its feet, the source of life; it depends on her in every fiber of its being. But it does not love her as a personal "Thou" either. Mother and child together form a primordial unity; they are bound to each other like the trunk and limbs of a body. But this unique relationship is only meaningful during the early years, and it must change gradually if the child is to develop properly. If the mother can regard her child as an independent person and treat it as such, then this mutual bond becomes transformed into love.

The bond can never be close enough; the mother loves her child so much she could "eat" it, and one of the things the child wishes for in his dreams is to re-enter his mother's body. However, love needs distance in order to develop; it must give the partner his freedom, so that it may be loved out of that freedom. The existence of a bond means that each desires to be as like the other as possible, as mother and child are alike, and little sisters, for instance, love to be similarly clothed. Love, on the other hand, seeks out what is personal and characteristic in the other and does its best to develop it, creating a safe, self-enclosed area in which the partner can be himself.

The longer the bond continues beyond the stage where it should have given place to this personal love, the more it is felt as bondage. Thence arise contradictory "ambivalent" feelings of pleasure in the bond, combined with a wish to be rid of it: mother and son are completely dependent on each other, yet never stop quarreling; have no wish to cause the slightest pain to each other, yet suffer boundlessly at each other's hands; are always full of concern and anxiety about each other and eaten up by silly fears about each other's health, yet do not understand how to make each other happy or even to let each other be happy on their own. This has been very accurately described as a "love-hate" relationship.

Bonds like this may exist not only between mother and

son but between father and daughter, or brother and sister. They are always a great obstacle to marriage; for they mean that the person concerned is not free to take a husband or a wife: the mother, or the sister, or the brother, is always interfering. Quite often both partners are bound to their families, and these are played off against each other. Every possible motive is brought in to intensify the bond: sentiment; childish gratitude; pity for poor mother; the need to support the unmarried sister; the feeling of reverence for wonderful dad; concern for the brother, who is still unable to stand on his own feet; etc.

Whatever form the attempt takes to bind the young husband to his family, there is only one reply to all this, and it is a dreadfully unsentimental one: "Therefore shall a man leave his father and his mother, and shall cleave unto his wife, and they twain shall be one flesh." No one is under any obligation to marry, but if he does then he must fulfill this basic requirement; otherwise there can be no marriage worthy of the name. The bond still existing between a newly married man and his mother, and her consequent interferences between man and wife, forms one of the most frequent causes of unhappiness in marriage. One of the most important fundamental rules of married life is that husband and wife shall never again employ the expression "my family," or "your family." These bonds should have been dissolved by the marriage, leaving only "our family." Such terms are always wrong, anyway, and only too likely to give offense.

A mother crowns her achievement in bringing up her son by transforming the bond between them into a love relationship that in fact makes him free for his future wife. He may seem less sentimental about her, may even now and again be rather rude to her, but this only means that his love for her will be more genuine and his gratitude more lasting.

The bond develops in the most puzzling way of all when it is unconsciously transferred from the mother or sister (or father or brother, as the case may be) to the wife or husband, who is then loved not "in married fashion" but "like a relation." The following are the chief symptoms of this substitution. The husband and wife are inseparable, yet are continually badgering each other. They believe that they must have the same attitude towards everything and cannot bear to have the other have an opinion of his own. One will grow depressed, to force the other to give in, and the other will sadly give way, so that the other will stop being sad. They are always thinking of every imaginable disaster that might occur to each other, and stifling each other with anxious attentions. True love, on the other hand, can bear separations, even long ones, and indeed grow as a result of them—reunions being cause for great celebration. True love allows the other his own opinion and lives by a harmony of opposites. It has faith in the other and trusts him, thinks lovingly of him in his absence, and regards his freedom as the highest of all goods.

Bondage as a substitute for love is also the most frequent cause of sexual upsets. A man who loves his wife as a child loves its mother or sister can never have a normally erotic attitude towards her. The usual results of an unconscious bond are either impotence or premature ejaculation; while the wife cannot give herself unreservedly to her husband as long as she is tied to him as if he were her father or her brother. Legitimate sexual feelings are thus divorced from love for the partner and it is then not love but a form of bondage which can no longer express a personal relationship. The sexual side element in the relationship becomes a mere material circumstance. The husband "takes" or "uses" the wife as if she were an object, the wife "puts up with" the husband. Sexual intercourse is brief, matter of fact, and automatic, and erotic feelings are accompanied by a sense of shame. Husbands who are "tied" to their wives can suddenly be overwhelmed with sudden "animal" lusts for other women, with whom they have no personal relationship at all. Such men become willing victims to the prostitute, that "woman without a face," and other attractions such as cover girls and chorus girls. Men tied to their wives in this way can neither desire women they respect, nor respect women they desire. Such bondage is a prison, whereas love is a liberation. It tries to force the other to conform to a pattern, whereas love leaves him free to become himself. It is impersonal, and therefore incapable of becoming erotic. It means clinging to the other and being selfishly possessive about him: it can never be near enough to him or long enough with him. Whereas love is satisfied with loving.

Sexuality, Eros, and Agape

When we speak of love we must distinguish between three different aspects of it. Unfortunately these are often confused with or opposed to each other. Just as every human personality has a physical, a psychological, and a spiritual aspect (or dimension), so within the living organism or union of two persons in marriage there are three aspects—Sex, Eros, and Agape.

The physical aspect is known as "sex." This comprises all the directly biological functions and experiences, from fertilization to birth, and more particularly associated reflexes like erection (stiffening of the male organ), ejaculation (outpouring of the seed), orgasm (climax of sexual delight), and so on. Like all the other biological functions, sexuality does not focus on a person as such, but on a person seen only as a desirable object. My mouth waters at the sight of an apple quite irrespective of whether the apple belongs to me or not. Similarly, a certain excitement arises in a man at the sight of an unclothed woman quite irrespective of whether she is his wife or a stranger, or whether or not he loves her, or even whether or not he has the remotest intention of having anything to do with her. What attracts male sexuality is not personal compatibility but female sexuality in general, as is to some extent conveyed by the expression "sex appeal."

Sexuality is a self-centered activity. It does of course transcend individuality in so far as it aims at propagation, for which it requires someone of the opposite sex, but its immediate motive is egoistic—the satisfaction of lust, sensual desire. The other person is only a means to an end, a person whose feelings are not taken into account. It thus becomes possible to by-pass sexuality by silencing one's desires through manipulation of one's own body: What is known as "masturbation" is a *reductio ad absurdum* of the impersonal mechanism of pure sexuality.

It would be a mistake to try to use these facts to discredit sexuality, which carries out the task of procreation and is, therefore, as much a part of creation and just as much willed by God as the functions of digestion, respiration, and the circulation of the blood. But like these it is a part of a greater whole, and there is something unnatural about it when it is excited and experienced purely for its own sake. People who eat immoderately ruin their constitutions instead of building them up. The impersonality of sex gives it its stability. This makes it to some extent unaffected by the ebb and flow of psychological moods and helps to ballast the ship of wedlock if any high seas should happen to get up. But on the other hand it makes it a thing that is blind and deaf.

Eros, unlike sex, is concerned with the other person as a person. It is not woman in general who attracts a man erotically, but some particular woman with her own personal characteristics. The sight of certain parts of the female body may excite a man sexually, but erotically he is aroused by a laugh, or a gesture, or a certain tone of voice that seems to reveal the actual person concerned. In fact Eros is so concerned with laying bare the soul that it prefers the veiled to the exposed—as the fashionable world of that highly erotic century, the eighteenth, knew so well. Eros does all it can to bring out the specifically masculine or feminine characteristics of the personality. Grace and kindness, charm and delicacy on the one side, chivalry, courage, gentlemanly behavior, and attentiveness on the other—all these are, in the best sense of the word, erotic things.

Eros, being an activity of the human spirit, always implies a relationship between two people. It never aims at satisfying individual desire but at producing a relationship in which each will give pleasure to the other. Self-satisfaction is a feature of sex, which is a solitary thing, but Eros is never solitary, for it lives by partnership. Eros finds its fulfillment in the relationship of love. It gives pleasure to both partners at the same time, enables them to give themselves to each other, entering into each other, stilling their own egos for the sake of each other. But though it is thus capable of breaking the shell of individuality, there is also a possibility that a harder shell will subsequently grow up around the couple bound by Eros. Eros's great temptation is an *egoïsme à deux*.

Eros is at once an art and a game. Art and games do not pursue an object but exist for their own sake—unlike technical operations, which are merely a means to an end. So we speak of the art of love and the game of love-making. Some moralists take offense at these expressions. They conclude from them that Eros is lacking in seriousness, is trivial and, therefore, to be rejected. In their eyes sex justifies its own existence by ministering to procreation, and it is, therefore, a more or less technical operation. But in this connection we should remember that animals never produce any works of art and hardly ever indulge in play when they are fully grown, and that Eros in the sense of love-making is largely unknown to them, as is speech. Speech, art, playfulness, and Eros are all in fact positive characteristics that distinguish human beings from animals. All that the moralists will recognize as valid is the "beastly seriousness" with which a dog devours his bone or a bull propagates his kind.

It is one of the great misfortunes of our age that Eros is largely unknown and confused with sexuality, at least in the case of men. Most of what is commonly described as erotic is merely sexual, and even the things that many moralists condemn as erotic are sexual too. In a certain hush-hush type of moral teaching young men are left to fight their impulses alone and as a result never progress beyond the notion of love as a mere sexual impulse. What they need is to be educated beyond sex and up to Eros. They need to be shown that the object of their main interest—a woman's body—though not in itself by any means evil or unimportant, is far less interesting than is a woman as a whole person, body, mind, and spirit. But the spirit cannot emerge freely until the business of sex has been mastered. Most of the so-called repressions—masturbation, sex curiosity, exhibitionism, fetishism, sadism, etc.—are simply fixations of the struggle against sex, isolated and more or less repressed, and they can only be overcome by accepting sex and combining it with Eros. Most young men stop masturbating as soon as they fall in love with a real girl, and an erotically happy relationship is hardly ever disturbed by perversion.

The commonest infirmity in marriage is probably the underdevelopment of Eros. Most husbands are prodigies in sex but almost complete morons so far as Eros is concerned. And so their wives, who live more by Eros than by sex, become psychologically disillusioned and, therefore, physically repelled by their husbands. Sexual coldness—"frigidity" as it is called—in wives is an exact reflection of a non-erotic and merely sexual attitude on the part of their husbands and can only be cured by treating the latter first.

All too often what is called "sexual education" restricts itself to anatomy, physiology, and pathology, and omits psychology; it concerns itself exclusively with sex, and knows nothing of Eros. The same is true of experiences with prostitutes, which give a false idea of the relationship between the sexes since Eros has practically no place in them.

Through meeting girls on friendly terms, through talking, perhaps, with some sensible and mature married woman, a young man will gradually come to discover the need for sexual restraint if there is to be any proper erotic tension. Water pipes only work at full pressure when the sluices are in proper order, and the maximum electric current can be maintained only when the whole circuit is properly insulated. If a short circuit occurs—i.e. when there is no resistance to the flow of current—the power quickly falls to zero. Eros depends in exactly the same way on the mastery of physical sex. If a man is incapable of self-restraint, if he causes a "short circuit" by masturbation or ill-timed sexual intercourse, his erotic tension falls to zero. Young men—and older men too—must realize that they must control their impulses, not because these are bad things in themselves or that a lot of sexual activity might have serious physical consequences for them, but because they must keep the erotic tension high if they and their wives are to get the most out of it. Moral exhortations denouncing the sexual impulse express a fundamentally wrong point of view, and their effect upon young people is nil anyway. What these young people actually need to do is to learn the "art of love," as a thing willed by God. And in this matter, as in all others, there can be no art without discipline.

Love also has a third, spiritual, aspect, which for want of a better name I must call *Agape*. Sex has its center of gravity in the ego; Eros has its center of gravity in "us two"—the human couple; Agape's center of gravity lies beyond the human couple. Agape includes mutual responsibility, but also a further responsibility to a third party. It maintains loyalty between couples even when one party no longer desires to be loyal. "Fall but in love with me, loyal thou needst not be," sings Eros. But Agape knows that even in the best marriages there can be times when love ebbs and loyalty has to fill the gap.

Agape, as Brunner says, loves the other because he exists, not because of certain characteristics. A man loves his wife, not just her beautiful face; a woman loves her husband, not just his intellect. Thus Agape is not tied to sexual differentiation like sex and Eros. "There is no more male nor female, but all are one in Christ Jesus." So, too, Agape is the basis of friendship. As Montaigne said of his friend La Boëtie, "If I am bound to say why I loved him, I feel that the only answer I can give is—because he was he, and I was I."

But it would be a gross mistake to set up Agape and Eros against each other as two mutually exclusive opposites, or as though Agape was nobler and more "Christian" than Eros. Both are necessary elements in any good marriage. Every good marriage must be a friendship as well as a marriage. Husband and wife must think as much of each other, love each other, interest each other, just as much as two really good friends. But woe to the marriage that is only a friendship, only Agape! In every good marriage, too, husband and wife must love each other as passionately, go on making each other as happy, go on being as new a surprise to each other, as any pair of lovers who are "mad about each other." But woe to the marriage that is only passion, only Eros! There is no need to go into any further detail as to how a marriage ought to include what is sexual without confining itself to it.

But it may be said that just as sex must be mastered before Eros can develop, so Eros must be mastered if Agape is to develop. Erotic harmony can keep husband and wife unaware of deeper oppositions between them, or even of some prevailing spiritual vacuum. So it is good for erotic relations to recede into the background, for a time at least, so that husband and wife may come to know the full meaning of Agape.

Marriage, then, is a far greater thing than sex, and a

greater thing than Eros or Agape. But it is also a greater thing than all three of them put together. For a whole is always greater than the sum of its parts.

Married Love

Marriage is not only a spiritual thing; it is a matter of flesh and blood too. It is not only a work of art; it grows up amongst actualities. It exists not only for the purpose of propagation, but in its own right. Marriage is an absolute companionship, not only of husband and wife as they are today but of their whole past and future, and not only of husband and wife alone but as they exist before God.

Marriage is not founded on big words, or carried through on sublime thoughts, or nourished by passionate feelings; it grows up out of the actual fellowship of everyday life—out of "existence" as we say today.

Marriage begins when a man and woman decide to spend their lives together and make a public announcement of the fact. But as yet it is like a newborn child—a real person, but weak and in need of development. It takes years to develop fully. Like a child, too, it is not simply an assemblage of a number of parts—sex, Eros, Agape, loyalty, etc.; it is a whole from the very beginning. But it grows with every day and goes on developing, as God intended it to.

Husband and wife share enjoyable experiences and frightening ones; they share drudgery and ecstasy. A child is given to them: they stand in amazement by its cradle, and later when it takes its first step from its mother's to its father's arms. Then again they bend over it together when it is ill; it pants for breath, and the same terror grips them and their joint prayer rises to God. If one of them is ill, the other does the work of both; if unemployment comes, they learn to economize and discover ways of dealing with the situation together. At times, too, husband and wife come into conflict with each other. They cannot understand each other or put themselves in the other's place, or give way: harsh words are spoken and they both feel terribly lonely and miserable and bad-tempered. And then they discover that no one else can help them, and that they are each other's hearth and home; and they come together again, and are ashamed of their thick-skinned egoism, and throw another layer of it away, once and for all. Marriage grows with every sacred stirring that husband and wife feel together—out in the country, it may be, or listening to music, or reading the Bible—and with every kind word spoken in bad moments, and every burst of childish laughter.

Husband and wife share not only the past but the future too—their joint plans and hopes and anxieties, and the joint uncertainty of not knowing at morning whether they will be together again at evening. God holds them together in his hand.

Such is marriage, and it is indissoluble. And though moments may come when you long above all things to dissolve it, and though the law may allow this and the judge declare it to be so and all the world approve—nevertheless, you cannot cancel this joint experience or dissolve such an organic bond. You are involved in it with every fiber of your being, and so is your partner.

Marriage also keeps its validity when death and destruction break over the land. Like a strong tower in a storm, it means home to the man at the Front and to the prisoner of war, to the wife in the factory, and to the child among strangers. Even if it is never to be found again in time, it belongs to eternity.

Calm, tempestuous, holy, passionate, tender, mysterious, humble, imperious, in deadly earnest, yet full of the joy of life—such is married love.

This love, this bond, is used again and again in the Bible as the only simile adequate to express God's love of man and His covenant with His people. "As a young man marrieth a virgin, so shall thy sons marry thee: and as the bridegroom rejoiceth over the bride, so shall thy God rejoice over thee." Thus does Isaiah[1] put it, and other prophets speak in similar terms. Jesus repeatedly calls himself "the bridegroom," and Paul finds the meaning of the mystery of marriage in Him.[2]

Thus married love has the power to make God's love either credible or incredible. Married love and fidelity decide what picture wife or husband forms of God's love and fidelity.

[1] 62:5.
[2] Eph. 5:32.

2.

MEN AND WOMEN

All living things are divided into male and female and each needs a complement if it is to propagate new life. In the case of human beings, and human beings alone, this goes a decisive stage further in that husband and wife not only come together to propagate new life but grow together in a more personal sense to form a new kind of unity. This unity takes time to develop, however, for both the young husband and his young wife regard themselves as normal and any differences in the other as abnormal. So we must now try to discover in what way both are equally "normal" and have been created to polarize and complete each other.

Masculine Outlook and Feminine Outlook

Men and women are not only distinguished from each other by physical and psychological characteristics but differ both fundamentally and in all their details in much the same way as a picture by Rembrandt differs from one by Raphael. What is required is not that they should resemble each other but that they should mutually complete each other, creating a harmony rather than a unison. Our ability to see three-dimensionally depends on the fact that our eyes register slightly different images of the scene before us. We need both eyes if we are to see things in the round; everything becomes flat if we close one of them. In married life something of the same kind happens.

One of woman's chief tasks is to bear and rear children, and to enable her to meet this she has a natural relationship towards everything that has life or soul or unity. She even tends to regard inanimate objects as things possessing souls, and this gives her the key to the world of fairy tale. Man, on the other hand, whose vocation is to protect and feed the family, has a special relationship with inanimate objects, which he can take to pieces and put together again. And so he tends to treat living creatures as if they were machines too.

Women also grasp the connections of things as a whole, as a given natural growth, and so they have a conserving, and frequently a conservative, tendency; whereas men regard everything as a collection of parts to be taken to pieces and put together again. Men want to renew and improve the status quo and are quite ready to be revolutionaries. This ability to take to pieces and build up again is at the bottom of that typically male thing, logic. For men two and two are always four. For women, on the other hand, two and two are never exactly four but a little less or a little more according to circumstances. A man will upbraid a woman for her lack of logic but her mathematics are quite right in her own sphere—for every biologist knows that in living nature two and two never equal four. They only equal four in man's world—the non-living world.

Women also regard their own personalities as a single whole. Physical indisposition, tiredness, the weather, have only a slight effect on their mood, whereas more abstract influences can often cause headaches or an upset stomach. The monthly period also affects their mood and is affected by it. Men dismiss this as "hysterical," but closer understanding shows this psychophysical harmony to be a very sound form of defense; for men, in whom "soul" and "body" are more drastically separated, can ruin themselves physically without realizing it and go astray psychologically without suffering physically. They have less in the way of danger signals and brakes.

Women thus possess an instinctive self-assurance to a large extent lacking in men. They automatically know things that a man has to work for laboriously with his intellect; in critical situations they act more quickly than men, who depend more on routine.

This lack of instinctive poise gives men a peculiar feeling of inferiority. They feel women to be nearer the earth, with their feet on the ground, capable of grasping the whole of things while they themselves know only the separate parts. This aspect of the relationship between men and women has hitherto received scant attention and I shall deal with it in greater detail later.

Men and women both serve God in their own way. Women experience God's creative power in their own bodies as their child grows. They exist to guard and sanctify life; they know that life is God-given and cannot be produced by human will. So they are orientated towards the status quo and support it with all their might. Their motto is, "Behold the handmaid of the Lord; be it unto me according to thy word." Men, on the other hand, always work outwards. They long to get beyond the circle of living nature and create something new. They have some sort of image within them which they must make actual no matter what the cost. They are always ready to break down what has been built so as to have something bigger and better to look at.

Differences in Character

Besides the differences deriving from their sex, there are
other differences in men and women which form part of
their individual character. As experience shows that opposites attract each other and that husbands and wives who
suit each other are usually poles apart in character, I shall
deal with the matter briefly here, and advise anyone who
wants further detail to read the excellent and quite easy
little book on the subject by Plattner.

The first set of opposites is made up of people who tend
to look outwards (extroverts) and people who tend to look
inwards (introverts). Introverts fight shy of other people;
they are "reserved" and so often seem unemotional. They
have more talent for tact than they have for contact. Contact is for the extroverts, who are always telling you what
they feel and think; they thus touch people's hearts more
readily and are more likable. Introverts tend to think them
rather interfering and tactless. Extroverts are all of a piece:
they "wear their hearts on their sleeve." Introverts have
two layers, a shell and a kernel.

Kretschmer's pair of opposites agrees more or less with
all this, but not entirely. In his *Körperbau und Charakter*
he divides people into "cycloids," who can be subdivided
into three groups which are

1) sociable, goodhearted, friendly, good-natured;
2) vivacious, humorous, lively, hot-tempered;
3) quiet, calm, serious, gentle;

and "schizoids," who include people who are

1) unsociable, quiet, reserved, solemn (humorless),
   eccentric;

2) bashful, shy, sensitive, emotional, nervous, excitable, nature lovers, book lovers;

3) docile, good-natured, straightforward, even-
tempered, obtuse, dull.

It is also worth noticing that generally, though not invariably, cycloids are correspondingly plump and thickset in
build (pyknic) while schizoids are thinner and taller
(leptosomatic).

Jung distinguishes, besides the two fundamental types of
introvert and extrovert, two more pairs of types—thinking
and feeling types, and intuitive and experiencing types.
These are dealt with at great length in his book, *Psychological Types,* and are concisely summarized by Plattner.

As opposites are mutually attractive we often find a man
of the introvert-thinking type marrying a woman of the
extrovert-feeling type, and a woman of the introvert-
intuitive type marrying a man of the extrovert-feeling type.
The differences between them can lead to difficulties in
their relationships and they may even "get on each other's
nerves" at times—in the literal sense of the words. It is,
therefore, important to realize that such differences of
character follow a general rule and are a good omen so
far as marriage is concerned, and that like sex itself they
are designed to bring about mutual completion and a harmony of opposites.

Mutual Projection

Not only do people marry members of the opposite sex
with particular characters of their own, but, even more im-
portantly, they also project images onto their partners that
originate not in the partners themselves but in their own
minds. As I have already said, the husband tends to project
some of his mother's characteristics onto his wife, and
when he discovers that his wife is in fact herself and not

his mother he feels rather let down. The same thing may happen in the case of the wife. But it should be remembered that even in the best marriages husband and wife are always "father" and "mother" to each other to some extent, besides being a great deal else.

In addition to projecting real persons—mother, sister, father, and so on—onto their partners, people also project their ideals onto them. Every young man dreams of an ideal girl, and when he meets someone answering approximately to this figure he imagines he has found his one-and-only chosen mate and immediately endows her with all the virtues of his ideal. This is "love at first sight." Actually he doesn't love the girl as she really is at all; he doesn't even know her. What he loves is a mental picture of her—his "anima." As Goethe said to Eckermann, "My idea of women is not derived from what I have actually seen; it was either inborn in me or else it has grown up inside me in some unfathomable way." Similarly, Don Juan never knew what any woman was really like but went on looking desperately for his anima in woman after woman, never seeing any of them as they really were and never finding what he wanted.

An anima is to a certain extent "the pure essence of femininity," as the man sees this. As he gradually discovers the real woman that lies behind the anima projection he may feel let down and even, paradoxically, reproach her for being "unfeminine" because she has not come up to his expectations. But when he is a bit more mature he will thank heaven for having given him someone really new to him and in every respect superior to his dream.

There are, however, women of theatrical type who either consciously or unconsciously act on the principle that they ought to play the anima part that men expect of them and thereby hook them. They act as screens for men to project their animas on, and stifle their own personalities completely. The more simple-minded men regard such women as ultrafeminine and aristocratic; and, the major part of literature being written by men, an anima type of this kind may be fabricated and thus impose a false picture of what a woman ought to be on a wide range of people, including women. This is the kind of woman who usually breaks up a marriage if the husband is not mature enough to love his wife as she really is.

The anima may be regarded, as Jung regards it, as a man's own feminine attributes suppressed into the unconscious. The more he has cut these off from his own personality and believes himself to be "a hundred per cent male," the less chance there will be of his realizing that when he sees his anima in a woman it is a projection of himself, and the more completely he will fall a victim to it.

A woman's masculine attributes suppressed into the unconscious are likewise called the "animus," and corresponding animus projections may be observed in women. But since the attributes are now male the animus consists not so much of feelings as of convictions and opinions, and one may often see even intelligent women holding firmly and quite uncritically to preconceived opinions which have their origin in the animus in precisely the same way as men regard their anima projection as an especially authentic type of womanhood.

Anima and animus, referring as they do to the opposite sex, are attractive projections, but other attributes of a different type which have been suppressed into the unconscious may also be projected onto the partner. These are known as "shadows." The man who is by temperament domineering and quarrelsome but who, as a result of his moral upbringing, has suppressed these attributes and cut them off from his conscious self tends to project them as shadows onto his wife and thus comes to regard her as domineering and quarrelsome. In quarrels between married persons it is quite a normal thing for husband and wife to reproach each other for bad qualities which they themselves possess, but in a suppressed form, so that they imagine they see them as shadows in the other.

In all cases in which husband and wife are hopelessly at odds with each other and see each other quite differently from the way they see themselves it is advisable to call in a marriage counselor who knows something about psychology and can look into the unconscious projections that have been made by both parties.

"Head" and "Heart"

"The husband is the head of the partnership," declares the Swiss Code of Civil Law, and it can find support for this in the Bible. Many men stick out their chests at having such a dignity attributed to them and many women feel degraded and injured by it, but the words are not really intended to form a basis for any attitude of superiority but simply to designate the husband as coxswain of the marital boat: He represents the association in the outside world, decides where to live, provides the bread and butter. These functions derive from his particular gifts and are nothing for his wife to get jealous about. Besides the "head," the marriage also possesses a "heart"—the wife. "She gives her man support with counsel and deed . . . she is the keeper of the house"—and, one may add, she plays the major part in bringing up the children. The husband designs the shape, the wife gives it body; the husband steers the boat, the wife looks after the passengers; the husband is the hearth, the wife the fire in the hearth.

If this relationship is rightly understood there need be no "struggle for power" between husband and wife; they can both feel happy in fulfilling their own function with the help of the other. The frequent struggle for dominance which nevertheless does occur has unconscious roots which we must try to trace.

We saw at the beginning of this chapter that the husband generally suffers from a feeling of inferiority to his wife because her instinctive feelings give her a greater sense of assurance. He is, therefore, very sensitive to her criticisms—far more so than either realizes—and is afraid of arousing them. To avoid the possibility of criticism he often abdicates from his role of coxswain and hands the responsibility over to his wife. Then he compensates for this by adopting a domineering attitude and assuming dictatorial airs. The wife, for her part, also suffers from a feeling of inferiority towards her husband; this has connections with the way she has been educated and conventions still fairly widespread. The more these feelings of inferiority have been suppressed the more she tries to compensate for them by criticism, faultfinding, and depreciation of men in general and her husband in particular. Such is the background to the "struggle for power."

On the other hand, the more the husband accepts his responsibility and acts like one who is in the best sense the "head of the partnership," the happier the wife feels and the better she plays her part as its "heart." But she must give her husband the self-assurance he does not by nature possess; she must trust him even if at first he seems to fail her; she must "blow" him into shape—"inspire" is the Latin word for it—with her love and praise so that he becomes a satisfactory coxswain.

When the wife neglects this duty of praising and continually encouraging her husband, or actively depreciates him, then he feels like a child with her and sooner or later will find another woman who looks up to him and regards him as a proper man. At this point there is a very great danger of infidelity. Most divorces can be traced back to the fact that the husband felt himself to be inferior to his wife, and she accentuated this feeling, until another woman came along who knew how to make a "head" out of him.

Generally speaking, an undue disparity in strength of character between husband and wife is one of the most frequent causes of misery in marriage. When the wife is stronger, more sensible, more experienced and spirited than the husband and takes care to let him know it, this usually leads to unhappiness and quarreling. When on the other hand the husband accepts his full share of responsibility as "head of the family" and the wife is the "heart" whose beat fills the whole house with living warmth, then the best foundation of future happiness has been laid for parents and children as well.

Choosing a Mate

A list of all the factors desirable for a successful marriage would make it seem an extraordinarily difficult matter to choose the right person. Fortunately most of us have the right feeling about this once we have come to realize how necessary it is to resist both feelings of infatuation and the contrary tendency to be overprudent and act from purely rational motives—and provided we always keep in mind that in entering upon marriage we are performing one of the most important acts of obedience to God.

Let me try, as briefly as possible, to indicate the main points here.

Erotic love alone, especially "love at first sight," is not a sufficient foundation for marriage; it sees only one side of the personality, and with eyes inevitably blinded by various projections. It never lasts long unless gradually taken into the context of love in the full sense of the word.

Purely rational marriages for family or professional reasons or based on community of interests are to be rejected if they run counter to erotic feelings. However, one frequently does come across marriages that have been decided upon "rationally," and in which erotic feeling has gradually grown up afterwards, which have proved very happy marriages indeed, whereas the great majority of avowedly "unreasonable" love-marriages turn out badly. Tagore says of marriage in India, "One cannot rely on spontaneous love to attain the ends of marriage . . . so from a girl's earliest years the idea of a husband is kept before her mind . . . the object of this is to substitute the refined sensibilities of married love for the natural passions of sex."[1]

The wife must be able to look up to her husband, so it is not a good thing if she is stronger, more passionate, more clever, more highly educated and experienced, or substantially older than he is. The husband for his part must be able to respect his wife as a person, so it is well for her to have more kindness, more refinement of feeling, more aesthetic taste and intuition than he has. So let a man ask himself if such and such a girl is really capable of becoming the "heart" of his family and let the girl test the man as to his fitness to be the "head." Headless or two-headed organisms are incapable of life, and marriage is an organism.

Marriage ought not to be undertaken blindly but with both eyes wide open; therefore, one must be on one's guard against all projections (anima, mother, sister, fairy-tale princess and so on) and idealizations ("I will only look at his good side") and try to see the other person as he or she really is. And, to show the other side of the picture, one ought not always to appear to the other person in one's "Sunday clothes" but as one's natural uninhibited self.

Everyday habits in such matters as clothes, recreation, eating, and other physical habits ought not to be overlooked or undervalued for they could hardly matter more. "Love is stronger than death, but a bad habit can often prove stronger than love," as Maria von Ebner-Eschenbach has said.

It is just as well to have seen the other person in a bad mood or a quarrel, for these bring out unexpected sides of the character. A young man who spills a glass of claret over his girl's new dress or sits on her new hat will often learn more about her character than he would have done in ten nights' courting. And Benjamin Franklin once said, "Marriage without love leads to love without marriage."

[1] Keyserling, *Das Ehe-Buch*, p. 102.

One may well sacrifice one's life out of pity for another, but one should never marry for that reason. (Girls should take special note of this.) Marriage based on pity is a mirage which always takes its revenge on both the people involved. However strong an idealistic love they may feel for each other, no one should ever marry anyone to whom he or she feels no physical attraction. No one should ever marry anyone in whose company he feels bored or is afraid of feeling bored. No one should ever marry anyone who is unable to share in the things he or she holds most holy. No one should ever marry "in hope"—the hope that this or that unpleasant peculiarity will change for the better as the years roll by: one must either accept a person in full or sever relations with him. A sensible and virtuous wife says to her husband, "I love you just as you are, but I am hoping that you may become what God wants you to be."

Confessionally "mixed" marriages can create difficult problems. Persons who are indifferent toward their own confession should at least be aware of the problems of such a marriage. They may not realize what they are getting into. Even more, we should warn those whose strong loyalties to their own particular Church may make them feel that other faiths are heresies or mere superstitions. There are, however, exceptions when Christ stands in their midst with such living power that each partner, without deserting his own denomination, can accept the other's and be enriched by it. In any case, it is necessary that both should know and respect each other's creed.

The Roman Catholic Church used to require that children be brought up as Catholics to make a mixed marriage valid, but according to the *Matrimonii Sacramentum* instructions of March 1966, the non-Catholic marriage partner may be freed from such an obligation if it violates his or her conscience, and according to Johannes Feiner, at least some leading Catholic theologians have suggested that it should always be determined "in which confession the children would have the best opportunity to grow up as better Christians, considering the specific family circumstances." Certainly the partners of a mixed marriage should always strive to preserve close contact with the spiritual counselors of both confessions.

Even more difficult may be the culturally or racially mixed marriage, which always calls for very careful deliberation. The problem is not so much the potential of discrimination as the possible difficulties in establishing a truly spiritual fellowship. As Martin Luther King so well stated it: "I want the white man to be my brother, not my brother-in-law."

In any general inquiry as to the advisability of mixed marriages those in favor and those against will be found to more or less balance each other. Twice as many mixed marriages end in divorce as compared with marriages within the same denomination, but this seems to me to be due not to the mixture in itself but to the frequent religious laxity of those who contract them.

Kaufmann recommends the following four categories of mutual interest as being likely to lead to a good marriage—"intellectual and emotional compatibility, sexual compatibility, agreement in economic matters and harmony in domestic (parent-child) relationships." And he goes on, "Researches into the causes leading to divorce show that a marriage is hardly ever endangered when only one of the four great fields of common interest is weakly developed but that marriage begins to ail when there is too little community of interest in two or more of these categories."[2]

Are there any psychological tests which enable one to be sure of making a right choice? With a good graphological analysis, or a test on the lines of Szondi's method, or the consultation of an experienced marriage counselor it is sometimes possible to discover why two people find each other mutually attractive while at the same time it would never do for them to marry. One may get rid of some

[2] *Kranke Ehen*, p. 21.

doubts this way, but it is never possible to make a positive statement that two people will suit each other and give them a guarantee that they will be happy together. One should be especially on one's guard against astrology and fortunetelling.

During the period of "engagement" the young couple will talk frankly about their future life together and get to know each other more than superficially. If irreconcilable differences of opinion or really serious doubts arise in the process, there should be no hesitation whatsoever about breaking off the engagement. Better do that, serious as it is, than go into an unhappy marriage and even, possibly, a divorce. Most unhappy marriages would never have been entered into at all if the people concerned had heeded the thoughts they pushed to the back of their minds during the engagement period. This is also a reason for abstaining from sexual intercourse before marriage: it robs one of one's freedom. Erotic harmony can never be "tested out" by premarital relations any more than you can test a parachute by a twelve-yard jump.

In spite of all our rational convictions and all our love, marriage cannot but be a critical step, a venture, a leap into God's arms. Once it has been decided on one may well recollect Alain's words: "I have bound myself for life; I have made my choice. From now on my aim will not be to choose a woman who will please me but to please the woman I have chosen." Even after what may have been in and by itself a wrong choice a marriage can be made into a splendid thing if God gives the necessary grace. It does not matter so much what one is at the moment of marrying, as the extent to which one is ready and able to change and improve. The qualification we most need for this is humility. So I shall end this section by quoting a rather appropriate metaphor which shows that it is better to possess humility than to know all about psychology. Roland der Pury compares marriage to a man and woman dancing together on a high tightrope. They all have at least one fall, he says. Some break their necks when they fall, but husbands and wives who have faith fall into the net spread out to catch them—into the Grace of God. There they roll into each other's arms and then they can climb back onto the tightrope again.

3.

THE FELLOWSHIP OF LOVE

"Earthly Love"

Human beings, being fruitful and being made one flesh in marriage are not bleak moral demands of conscience. Nor are they mere unconscious impulses, like animal instincts. Human beings have been given a way in which they may fulfill God's command joyfully.

Always, however, men have been tempted to put apart the two things God has joined and to separate the commandment from the pleasure, so that either they seek the pleasure alone without love and fruitfulness, or they think of the commandment as a form of duty and sacrifice and regard the pleasure as a sin. In this way "heavenly" love is opposed to "earthly" love, as they are in Titian's picture, and man is split irreparably in two.

The fact is that people who make the sharpest distinction between "earthly" and "heavenly" love go either to one extreme, and renounce love and tenderness and warmth of feeling altogether, or to the other, where they are attacked by enormous and generally perverse sexual obsessions which are marked less by pleasure than by compulsion mania and evil. They provide a striking illustration of the truth of Pascal's saying: "Man is neither an angel nor a beast, and the sad thing is that the would-be angel becomes an actual beast."

What we need to do, in contrast to all this, is to look for a human equilibrium, the place where heaven and earth touch each other and spirit becomes flesh. It is not only children that are generated by the act of love. The fellowship of marriage is also created by the husband and wife becoming one flesh. Here loving becomes living, in its most vital sense, for it involves the whole personality. When love brings this about, the shell of the ego is burst apart and freely opened to the other person; then two lives actually flow into each other and the two become one flesh.

On the other hand, anyone who performs this act without love does produce an imitation of some of its phases but lacks the most decisive factor in it—the opening of the I to the Thou, and what goes with it, the becoming one flesh. This cannot take place merely as the result of the union of two sexual organs but only through the loving unification of two personalities. This needs to be impressed both upon the "moral" people who think that marriage is consummated in the wedding ceremony, and also upon the "immoral" ones who imagine that they can prepare for marriage by previous "sexual experience." The latter are in fact in danger of missing the decisive experience altogether, the main concern of all the previous preparations for marriage, because their ego has become insensitive to Eros.

This should serve to show what an exalted thing pure erotic experience is, and how sharply it is to be distinguished from the impulsive automatic intercourse of animals.

The Art of Love

The more the erotic experience rises above mere sexuality and assumes a form in which the whole personality is concerned, the less can we rely on "natural instinct." Natural instinct is only a groove surviving from past ages; we need to get out of it and develop beyond it. The peculiarly human elements in erotic experience are freedom and the capacity to create something new. This makes it a work of art, and creates between it and the intercourse of animals a distinction similar to that which exists between a piece of architecture and a bird's nest or a molehill.

Every art has to be learned. A bird can rely on instinct in building its nest, but not an architect. Neither can the man who wants to make his marriage a work of art. It may be thought bad taste to mention this. Nevertheless, the majority of the men who imagine they can rely on their "nature" remain bunglers and their wives soon learn that this boasted "nature" is—like all merely instinctive things—bestial.

There are two great prerequisites to the art of love: 1) an elementary knowledge of the structure and function of the sexual organs, and 2) a realization that marriage is a great deal more than a mere matter of sex. This knowledge must be acquired during the engagement, if not before, and certainly before the first sexual approaches are made; and it is first and foremost a matter for the man, since it is his job, as we have said, to be the "coxswain."

In the next few sections I shall summarize the bare essentials of this knowledge. It is a good thing to read something on the subject, but nothing takes the place of personal contact with the other sex—such as we find in the comradeship of groups of young people of both sexes—or what a young man can get from friendship with a mature married woman. Let me here say emphatically that I am not referring to any physical relationship, but to intellectual friendship and comradeship. Such friendships demand complete control over one's sexual feelings, the very thing which is the second prerequisite of the art of love, upon which I wish to put special emphasis.

The most important thing in the art of love is to realize that it does not consist only in a "technique," but that there can be no sexual happiness without Eros and no erotic harmony without Agape. To seek to satisfy one's own impulses is not an art at all, whereas it is very much an art to know how to ensure that both partners *together* experience the greatest possible happiness and thereby feel the deepest intimacy with one another. Art means not only fulfilling the requirements of nature, but going beyond them to the creation of something new, personal, and never previously existent.

The demands this makes upon a husband are very practical indeed. Do not expect your wife to show any close affection when she is not in the proper mood; do not wish for sexual intercourse if there is reason to foresee that your wife will find it disappointing; do not proceed to the act itself until your wife is in the right psychological condition (a thing for which you may have to provide for hours beforehand); do not insert your penis until your wife has been sufficiently excited by the preliminary love play; postpone your ejaculation as long as possible so as to increase the pleasure for both of you to the greatest degree; do not go to sleep as soon as it is over but keep up your interest in your wife during the subsequent play. Before marriage it is best to keep every sort of sexual excitement towards your fiancée under complete control since it is not good for her. Towards any other woman keep erotic excitement so much under control that she does not notice it at all, for it could lead to unfortunate results between you.

The art of love may lead within marriage to complete abstention for long periods, e.g. during the absence or illness of the partner or by mutual consent for the purpose of internal concentration and maturing. It means the widest possible freedom from animal lust, so as to be free to love one's partner and make him or her happy. And it means freely renouncing all absolute demands for satisfaction and ceasing to believe in the compulsive character of the impulse. It means surrendering one's whole sexuality to God, so that He may use the two people involved to create something new.

Since van de Velde's celebrated book, which did perhaps fulfill a contemporary need, opinion has become widespread that the art of love consists in the knowledge of as many artifices and variations of erotic union as possible, and continual change has been regarded as the surest way of keeping a marriage from becoming a bore. One may admit that there is no objection to variation and refinement of technique, but one must also insist that it will be disastrous for anyone to rely on them to put new life into marriage! To illustrate what I mean let me say that it is a good thing for a housewife to make sure of plenty of variation in the diet but it would be a fundamental mistake for her to imagine that she can keep her husband faithful to her by change of diet alone, for it is precisely the stay-at-home husband who gets the most pleasure from going to a little restaurant now and again. Whereas if the wife manages to create an atmosphere of ease and gaiety, humor and affection, at her table, then she can set potatoes and white coffee in front of him every day and he will never feel any need to go anywhere else for his food. It must of course be added that half raw or oversalted potatoes are quite capable of diffusing gloom where previously the atmosphere had been good!

The art of love consists in distinguishing things of major importance from things of minor importance and giving the former first place. This is as true of erotics as it is of money or housekeeping—none of which should ever be allowed to get in the way of love.

Finally, love consists less in doing than in being, less in

speech than in sympathy, less in anything that one gives out of oneself than in the simple fact of "being together and loving each other." The greatest enemy of love is lust, which wants to get something for itself and employs the other as a means of satisfying this want.

Passion and Affection

The erotic sensibilities of men and women are as different as the rest of their natures: The man moves chiefly within the physical and the spiritual spheres, so he lives in sexuality and Agape, whereas the woman lives mainly in an intermediate plane and her experience takes the form of Eros. Of course these contrasts are not absolute, but in practice they are important enough to be opposed to one another in the way suggested here.

The man lives in the atmosphere of his profession during the greater part of the day and hardly even thinks of love, and when he returns home it takes him a considerable time to get into an erotic atmosphere—which, like many other more mature feelings and emotions, can only come about gradually. But he can be very quickly aroused sexually by some very minor attraction and then feel intense sensual desire—generally mistaking this for being in the right mood from a purely erotic point of view. The chief difference between the two things is that, as was shown at length above, Eros is something in which the couple are both concerned, so it works by contagion, one partner catching it from the other. Sex, on the other hand, is a purely biological affair which only affects the single individual. If Eros does not precede sex, preparing the way for it in the woman's soul, its outward manifestations can be highly offensive to her. Whereas Eros charms and sets free and bestows happiness, all sex can do alone is to subdue by force. This leads to a situation, as common as it is tragic, in which the husband displays intense sexual desires and finds his wife more frigid and reluctant every time.

The wife for her part does not have her whole attention taken up by professional or domestic problems in as one-sided a fashion as the husband; but in any normal marriage she lives with a more or less constant feeling about him. "All the thoughts of my heart are always of thee." This usually produces a faintly erotic atmosphere which only wants a nod from the partner to burst into full flower. But if these "thoughts of the heart" are negative, then an erotic obstruction is inclined to arise which it is no easy matter to overcome. The wife's state of mind when her husband leaves her as he goes out in the morning is in most cases determinative of the success or non-success of the love-making in the evening. Thus everything depends on whether the wife is successful in gradually bringing her husband into the right erotic mood, out of which sexual activities will flow in a way harmonious for them both, or whether the naked unerotic sexual demands of the husband kill the wife's faint erotic tendency instead of making it burst into flower.

What the wife requires first, last, and all the time is affection. To her the connotation of this word is entirely nonphysical. It is suggested in the tone of voice in which her husband says good morning to her, the look in his eyes as he passes her the coffeepot, the attitude he takes to protect her if the need arises. The affection for which the wife longs is like an invisible mantle in which her husband wraps her and in which she feels secure. For her, affection is a noun summing up everything which gives her the feeling of being on intimate terms with her husband.

But when the husband speaks of being affectionate (he almost invariably uses the word as an adjective) he usually means bodily caresses, which are usually only the prelude to fuller union. So as long as the day's work lasts he has "no time to be affectionate," and when he has time he immediately gets down to business. The two are poles apart from each other: the husband "gets affectionate" at specific times and does it in a sexual way and stops feeling affectionate as soon as he has given vent to his passions; whereas the wife's affection covers the whole of her time—a coat with holes in it keeps no one warm—it is erotic in nature and forms the basis and indispensable prerequisite to sexual passion, if there is to be any. As a result of this the union of love must, if the wife is to take part in it at all, grow up out of an erotic and, therefore, psychological atmosphere. This mood must have been properly prepared often for hours beforehand; a trifle—a rough word or over-assertive gesture on the part of the husband, moral disappointment with him, or any other such cause of annoyance —may rudely upset the wife's erotic mood.

The husband, on the other hand, can feel sensual desire without being erotic in mood. In fact, it is just because he is not in an erotic mood that he feels "sensual desire." Any external or internal attraction serves to awaken his sexual appetite; he wants satisfaction and wants it to be as soon, and as quickly over as possible. So he sets his course for his goal and by strong uncontrolled movements quickly reaches the zenith of passion, after which passion may drop quickly to zero or even enter a negative phase in which he feels exhausted and sinks into a deep slumber. There is hardly any change of mood as great or as sudden as the husband's before and after union, if that mood is determined by sexuality alone.

The wife feels things quite differently. Her physical and sexual sensations develop only gradually out of her erotic ones. This gradual rise of passion is in itself the greatest of pleasures, so she would prefer it to last as long as possible, while the climax of her orgasm is not the objective of the whole act in as pronounced a way as it is in the case of the man. It is more like the summit of a gradual ascent. Afterwards the woman's feelings do not sink at once to zero as with the man, but slow down very gradually before stopping, and this gradual descent from the heights is particularly important and pleasurable for a woman. But it only feels natural to her, if she experiences it in common with her husband; if he at once falls asleep, the wife feels that she has been defrauded of something important; still more so if he has passed his climax while she is still working towards hers.

When expressed in the form of a graph, the curve representing the man's sexual pleasure rises steeply to its climax and falls still more steeply after it, whereas the woman's both rises and falls gradually. The most important thing to aim at is that the two summits should approximately coincide. But a hardly less important objective is the widening of the man's pleasure curve; in other words, he should always be trying to extend the duration of the union. Orientals, who are much more sophisticated in this sphere than Occidentals, employ all their arts to make the union last as long as possible, so as to give the greatest happiness to both husband and wife. This, translated into our terms, means that the husband must ever keep trying to be more and more erotic, instead of only sexual, in his feelings, and that he should leave more and more room for affection as compared to passion; if he does so he will discover that a sexual passion not inferior to a man's can awaken in his wife, and make them one both erotically and sexually.

In order that this unity may be brought into being, there is need of the third element, Agape. The union, with its affection and passion, must not be an isolated thing torn out of its context within the whole marriage. Husband and wife must not enact by night something which does not enter their consciousness by day. Concretely expressed: the husband displays his chivalry—a quality in men which women specially value—by controlling his passions at every moment and putting them completely at the service of mutual experience. So the animation of the games, or conversation, or music during the evening will often create an erotically affectionate atmosphere. Perhaps that will be all, and husband and wife will go to sleep feeling happy and the better for it. Or perhaps both husband and wife—it must be both—will recognize the distant surge of passion in the atmosphere and, under the continual guidance of love, unite with each other completely.

The art of love consists in refusing to let oneself be carried away by blind impulse, and instead making impulse take the shape of a shared experience.

"Technique"

What has been said so far should have made it clear that the decisive thing about uniting in love is not technique but psychological attitude, erotic atmosphere, the very fact of being there and loving each other. When these are absent, all the technique in the world can cause nothing but suffering. Yet experience also shows that a bad technique can disturb true love so that the union is not greatly enjoyed and may even be a torment to one or both parties. For these reasons I must now go on to the most important aspect of this matter, which every husband ought to understand. St. Clement of Alexandria says in this connection, "We need not be ashamed to call by their proper names things which God was not ashamed to create."

When a newly married couple come to spend their first night together, both are in a state of glad excitement about what is going to happen between them, but along with this gladness there is also generally mingled a little anxiety. The young man wonders if he will be able to manage properly; the young woman often has no very precise idea of what exactly is going to happen to her; she is perhaps afraid that she will not be able to help feeling embarrassed, or otherwise behaving foolishly, and perhaps she is also suffering from an elemental physical anxiety before this new experience. Both, therefore, should have this deeply impressed on their minds: "Your great expectations will not all come true tonight; this will only be a modest beginning. It is not of much importance how far you get when you begin tonight: all your life lies before you, to get on further; but on the other hand, it is all important to begin in the right way."

The young woman must be assured beforehand that her husband will not make an unconditional demand of her to have "everything" all at once, but that if it proves necessary he will be satisfied to lie beside her and chat to her and admire her. A chivalrous man's first virtue is self-control. Any man who demands from his bride a stage of intimacy for which her heart is not yet ready commits a rape upon her, and any man who merely "enjoys" her as if she were an object repudiates from the beginning the erotic relationship, and perhaps by that lays the foundations of a frigidity which will last on through the whole marriage. And even if they do attain full union both should realize that the highest pleasure has not yet been attained, particularly in the case of the woman, any more than a young man who gets a violin for Christmas can move his audience under the lighted tree to tears the first time he plays it. The virgin who has had no previous experience may have a strong desire for affection, her whole body can be eroticized, but her specifically sexual feelings are still weak and will take some few weeks or months to reach full maturity. So the young husband should not take for granted what does not as yet exist; he should not take in a single jump what he ought to take in several successive stages, and he must keep continually in mind that every untimely sexual exaction causes a corresponding defensive reaction.

The union of love may be divided into three phases, each of which should be clearly distinguished from the other two: the love-play (prelude), the actual intercourse, and the afterplay. Contrary to what usually is believed by males, the second phase is not without qualification supreme, but each of the three phases has an independent significance of its own, and no one of them can exist without the two others. Referring to the union of love the Bible says, "Adam knew Eve his wife." It is impossible to define it more appropriately: Every time husband and wife should know each other afresh and know each other more deeply, physically, psychically, and spiritually. If the union does not lead to such knowledge, it remains nothing more than a stimulation and subsequent release of impulse, it remains a habitual courtesy granted from time to time, it remains the "conjugal rights" conceded with resignation. If the union is failing to show its full significance it might be better to do without it altogether.

Love-play consists in a progressive and partly symbolic uncovering of the wife, an uncovering of her inner self more than just of her body. The playful resistance of the wife is overcome not by the strength of the husband, but by his self-control and by the reassuring attentiveness of his love. He should win his wife afresh each time, not by technical tricks but by his whole attitude.

This attitude of course will also express itself by caresses; what form they should take should be gradually learned with affection, tact, and sympathy. It should be stated here that no touching or giving up oneself to be touched, however intimate, can be called "immoral" in itself, so long as it is not done merely for one's own satisfaction with the disapproval of one's partner but is really aimed at the other's happiness. The essential meaning of love-play is at once psychic and erotic: both husband and wife should feel that they belong to each other without any reserve, that they can make each other happy with their whole beings, and that their minds unite more and more in this artful edifice of talk and gesture.

The physical results at the end of the love-play should be that the husband's penis should be fully erect and the entrance to the wife's vagina sufficiently moist that an easy entrance is possible. Unless these two conditions are fulfilled it is senseless to attempt to come together; to do so will only lead to pain for the woman and bitter disappointment for the man. Under such circumstances one must at the very last moment be prepared to give up the prospect of full union and be ungrudgingly satisfied with the joys of love-play. It also, as has been shown, possesses a separate significance of its own and can by itself give happiness to husband and wife. The length of the love-play cannot be determined, but it should as a rule last more than five minutes.

Copulation begins when the husband inserts his erect penis into the wife's vagina. At first it is best to do it while the wife lies on her back, laying a small cushion under the small of her back and spreading out her legs comfortably with the upper thighs slightly bent. The husband does not just lie on top of her, but supports himself on his knees and elbows, so as not to weigh too heavily on her. The male organ is inserted from in front and above while, especially at first, the husband's or the wife's hand helps it to find its way. It must be realized that the opening in the woman's pelvis runs steeply up and backwards.

The first time they copulate the maidenhead (hymen) of the wife, which partly closes the vaginal passage, will be pierced, causing slight pain and almost imperceptible bleeding. There is no need whatever for any nervousness at this moment; still, the husband should remember that this first union usually does not give the same pleasure to his wife as it does to himself. If the exceptional occurs and the hymen is not penetrated after repeated attempts on different days, then after a week or so a gynecologist should be consulted. In a slight and painless operation, he can deal with the obstinate hymen. Whatever objections one may at first find to this solution, it is better than plaguing each other for whole weeks or maybe months and thereby perhaps sowing the seed of a permanent disinclination. It may be added that in older days an undue significance was ascribed to the hymen, not only in regard to the pleasure its penetration (defloration) was supposed to have for the man, but also in regard to its value as the sign and seal of virginity. In actual fact virginity has a psychological rather than an anatomical reference; that is to say, it consists in the inviolateness not of the hymen but of the feelings, and the same is true of the pleasure which a virgin gives her husband.

The art now consists in getting intercourse to last as long as possible. This is mainly because the pleasure curve of the wife rises more slowly, and therefore takes a correspondingly longer time to reach its summit; but it is not only for the sake of the orgasm but because being together like this is in itself full of pleasure and significance. The excitement of inserting the male organ creates a strong impulse to move it up and down within the vagina, a thing that is most pleasurable for both parties, but which brings about a premature outpouring of seed (ejaculation) and consequent relaxation of the penis. Ejaculation by itself cannot be controlled by the will but takes place automatically when sensual excitement has risen to a certain point. So if there is a desire to make intercourse last as long as possible, then all that can be done is to ensure that the excitement, especially at the beginning, does not develop too quickly. The husband must so far control himself as not to insert his penis too deeply, and above all not to indulge in any vigorous movement of it (friction) until after the first wave of excitement has died down. Necessarily he must lie perfectly still every now and then. The longer intercourse lasts, the less excitable he is, so after waiting a few minutes he can carry out the strong movements of friction which bring to its climax the pleasure of both parties and feel he has not lost anything by it.

How long should intercourse last? At least until the wife has reached her climax of pleasure, the technical name for which is "orgasm." However, it will be a good thing if the orgasm can by skillful control be postponed as long as possible so as to make the two partners relax and melt into each other still more completely. According to the great statistical inquiry made by Kinsey, which also is supported by Stone, actual intercourse lasts on the average between one and two minutes among modern Americans. This would seem a ridiculously short time to an Oriental, and indeed it is much too short for most women to attain to an orgasm. So they are condemned by it to remain unsatisfied, a thing which should be avoided, or else get some release subsequently by continuing the conditions of intercourse by means of the finger. That may be better than nothing, but is far from being an ideal solution. Among a great many men, too, ejaculation takes place a few seconds after the insertion of the member. In many cases it even takes place previously, so as to make the insertion no longer possible. This is what is termed premature outpouring of semen (ejaculation praecox). All authorities are agreed that this disturbance is one of the chief misfortunes to a marriage; yet, strange to say, most of them fail to tell us how to get rid of it. So we are compelled to go more deeply into the problem, the more so insomuch as the practice we shall recommend is addressed not only to the matter of premature ejaculation but can be of general service in once more extending the clumsy sexual intercourse of the "West" and making it into a genuine act of erotic fellowship in the Oriental manner.

Quick outpouring of seed is partly a regression to mere animality; since most animals, having no knowledge of Eros, proceed to ejaculation, which is all that is necessary to secure fertilization, after a few seconds. Partly also it is a result of male egoism, which rushes blindly towards its goal without thought of the female partner. Finally, paradoxically enough, it is often the symptom of an obstruction caused by a subconscious bad conscience about pleasure. The subconscious mind of the man who has been imprisoned in a certain rigid type of morality says more or less, "Since I can't help doing it, then let it be done as quickly and pleasurelessly as possible." Accordingly the basis and first step towards recovery consists in an internal change-over from animal sex to human Eros. To have Eros, you must have a couple. So quick and pleasureless ejaculation ought not to be designated as the "more moral" of the two but as merely bestial. The mere transference of attention from his own pleasure to that of his female partner will be enough to bring about a considerable extension of the period of intercourse for many a man.

Also, the husband should avoid at first all vigorous movements or deep insertion of his penis, fill his lungs with air as much as possible, hold his breath, hold in his stomach, and stretch the muscles of his pelvis (by pulling in his posterior). An Indian artifice described by Chanson can be of great service also. If the husband keeps vividly imagining the direct opposite of what is actually happening, and thinking that his penis is fulfilling its function by sucking in instead of pouring out, then he will hold back the natural ejaculation reflex. To increase the vividness, he should make a picture in his mind of this "backwards flowing stream" as evaporating over a little flame, which he should think of as burning behind his bladder. By dint of constant practice this paradoxical conception can effect an extraordinary retardation of ejaculation. But it takes time and patience, and both parties should not begin at too early a stage to lose heart or renounce their efforts. On occasion the rubbing of the gland, especially the pad at the back of the penis, with an anesthetizing ointment such as Nupercainal half an hour before intercourse can retard ejaculation.

Once success has been obtained in making intercourse last some few minutes, then the rest depends to a certain extent on what the husband chooses to do—on how much longer he holds himself in, when he sets off the orgasms of both, engaging in some particularly strong and vigorous friction resulting in ejaculation for himself and at the same time producing the orgasm in his wife. Her orgasm expresses itself by rhythmic contractions of the vagina, the pelvis, and indeed of the whole body, but consists above all in a quite uncontrollable sensation of pleasure, often leading to a slight feeling of faintness.

At the beginning of copulation, the clitoris, a pea-sized thickening above the entrance to the vagina, is especially erogenous. After insertion, the erogenity is transferred to the walls of the vagina, and this should lead to a deep, climactic orgasm. If it doesn't occur, the woman can increase her readiness by the exercise of rhythmic contractions (pulling in the posterior) during the daytime.

After the climax the tension relaxes quickly in the man but slowly in the woman. If the man now gives in to his animal impulse to turn away from his female partner and go to sleep, as so frequently occurs, then the woman at this her most exquisite moment feels herself abandoned and alone, takes a long while to calm down, and has then anything but friendly feelings towards the man. It thus comes to pass that many a husband is surprised the morning after sexual intercourse to find his wife in a bad mood.

So here should begin what is so often neglected—the afterplay. On the purely animal plane the man feels rather flat, and even depressed ("Omne animal post coitum triste"), but insofar as his feelings are not merely sexual but also erotic he opens up his heart to his wife in a special way just at this very point.

After the storm of passion the two lovers are intimately opened up to each other, and can look straight into each other's souls. The happiness they have just experienced fills them with deep gratitude to each other and to God for giving them such a partner. They can now say and reveal to each other things which would not otherwise find expression, problems are solved without saying a word, and they now experience what full fellowship can mean. And at this moment the Biblical phrase "Adam *knew* his wife" finds a spiritual fulfillment as well. The enormous vital energies of intercourse have not simply vanished like so much smoke; they have transformed themselves instead into spiritual love: in fact all that generation of power was required so as to bring about this incredible manifestation of full fellowship.

External Conditions

I have referred already to the importance of being in the right erotic mood, particularly in the case of the wife. This especially means that intercourse for her cannot mean peace after a serious quarrel as it often can for the husband. A woman cannot generally change her mood as quickly as that, and when the husband approaches her with such a suggestion it only makes the quarrel break out again. "First you make little of me, then all I'm good enough for is—that! It's your only reason for making up with me." Love is never a means to an end, not even peace, but carries its meaning within itself.

The external setting also plays a part in inducing the right mood. The bedroom should be furnished with taste, which does not necessarily mean luxury. It should as far as possible be isolated from the other bedrooms. Children, even comparative infants, should never sleep in their parents' bedroom. The wife will feel most uneasy if she has reason to fear being overheard by her children or even her mother-in-law. The room itself should be dimly lighted. While bright lighting has a disturbing influence on the wife, complete darkness prevents people from looking at each other—and it is of great importance psychologically to be able to do so. It should be observed here that the sight of his wife's lightly clothed or naked body has a very great erotic charm for the husband, and any prudery about this on the part of the wife is totally out of place. (That there is also a charm in covering and uncovering, and that it is possible to exercise tact without being a prude is another story.) The naked male body, on the other hand, has not as a rule a similar effect on the wife; in fact the very sight of it may under certain conditions cause a disinclination for closer contact. So the husband should show discretion about how he undresses. If the wife has noticed that the husband appreciates some particular feature of her dress, some ornament or perfume or even lipstick, she should use this knowledge to good purpose. In this connection I must mention the importance of scrupulous cleanliness, which involves at least a daily washing of the feet and the area round the sexual organs. An unpleasant odor can quite annihilate the most exquisite of moods, as also can a bristly beard.

The love union itself is capable of endless variations. Once both have attained to some success while the wife lies on her back, they can gradually experiment and discover new positions. It is worth calling particular attention to the position in which the woman is astride the man while he lies or sits, a position which was normal in ancient times and still is in certain regions and which will be found exceptionally enjoyable by both parties. All that need here be said on the subject is to emphasize that such variations are in no way improper as long as they express mutual love and are not employed by one party—generally the man—in order to make an impersonal "use" of the other. The truth is the direct opposite: the "good-natured habit," performed apathetically as a routine matter, may be described as loveless and therefore in the highest degree immoral because it is boring to the partner instead of making her happy and is not bestowed as a gift but demanded as a "conjugal right." But it is important to remember that technique alone can never make a happy marriage. There are some married couples who manage things very awkwardly and yet succeed in being happy.

No hard and fast rules can be laid down as to the frequency of intercourse. The rule ascribed mistakenly to Luther—"twice a week, making a hundred and four a year" —may strike an average, but nothing is more mistaken than to treat this matter like a railway timetable. There are times when both require daily unions and times when pauses of a week or a fortnight are desirable. The more passionately inclined partner must in any case let the quieter one set the pace, just as on a walking tour it is the long-legged walker who lets the shorter-legged companion determine the speed, and not the other way round. Many a marriage which began well erotically has been spoiled through the husband's being inclined toward too many unions and the wife becoming frigid as the result of being forced when she had no appetite. It must be admitted on the other hand that too slow a rhythm, that is one with intervals of two or three weeks, is unpropitious when it follows not natural inclinations but a doctrinaire set of rules. It takes love, tact, and maybe even cunning to know how to stir up the less passionate partner erotically—not sexually! On the other hand the more passionate one should not be met with a brusque refusal (accompanied when occasion offers by some moral reflections). He or she should be given to understand in the most affectionate way that the union will be fuller and richer in a few days' time. Finally it should be said that it often happens, especially with youthful couples, that before they realize it the afterplay has become the prelude to a fresh union. In a long and completely happy union the lovers will have put so much into the act itself that as a rule repetition seems scarcely either possible or desirable. At times, however, union may last only a short time, perhaps after a long separation and holding back of feeling, and the proper mutual bestowal of happiness will not come until a second union a quarter or half hour afterwards.

The happier and more mature a marriage is, the less does sexual impulse set the pace. Instead, intercourse becomes the expression of a complete love for each other as persons and guided by God. Intercourse which does not proceed from this love will be felt to be loveless. Indeed, in certain circumstances love can seek quite a different means of expression and do without physical union altogether. It is no longer impulse or self-will that is in command but God's personal guidance. Admittedly it is no easy matter to respond to this, but is that any reason for not attempting to? Simple recipes are almost always risky.

Usually it is assumed as axiomatic that the husband alone should be active and that it is the wife's part to remain in a state of passiveness. This is a mistaken prejudice. The traditional caricature of man's role is of course that of the "cave man." But has not woman's role as "vamp" just as long a history behind it? She has it to a great extent within her power to awaken and educate her husband's Eros by the way she behaves. Gentlemanliness is a man's response to, his reflection of, a woman's grace; and a harsh and school-mistressy attitude on her part will only awaken the naughty boy in him. Many men greatly appreciate affectionate caresses, especially when they are getting older. So if the wife finds he likes it, she should not be shy of taking hold of his penis and stroking it very gently. Statistics show that many men develop a feeling of inferiority when they find their sexual vigor decreasing a little between the ages of forty and fifty and are pleasantly surprised when an active woman shows that she knows how to reawaken their powers. Which is better—for such a man to find such a woman outside the home, maybe even in a public house, or for his own wife's skill to succeed in restoring his self-confidence?

Obstacles to Intercourse

During the first few months of marriage, the sexual potency of the husband is frequently disturbed and it is more or less usual for the wife to feel little pleasure. So they should not lose heart at once but remember that every art must be learned by practice.

Even in the happiest marriages intercourse can occasionally prove unsuccessful, so there is no need to take this as a tragedy. We speak of "frigidity" only when the wife permanently fails to find any pleasure in erotic fellowship. The obstacle is only relative if, while feeling erotic inclinations, she is averse to actual intercourse, or if, in the slighter form of it, she does feel a gradual rise of sexual pleasure but cannot reach a proper orgasm and the subsequent release of tension. In the worst cases, at the husband's approach the vagina closes up so tightly as to prohibit all entry. The technical name for this difficulty is *vaginism*.

The causes of frigidity may vary greatly. The physical causes are the rarest: underdevelopment, swollen glands, general fatigue. The causes are much more often psychological: a narrow-minded upbringing, by which all that is erotic has been suppressed and driven into the unconscious; feelings of guilt or inferiority as a result of experiences in childhood or masturbation or lascivious fantasies; an unconscious fixation on the father, brother, or a former lover; anxious fears of the male and unconscious resistance to playing her part as a woman; but most frequently wifely frigidity may be traced back to wrong behavior on the part of the husband—insufficient love-play, premature outpouring of seed, a demanding instead of a wooing attitude, or a wrong choice as to the time for intercourse to suit his own needs and not his wife's. To weigh all these possible causes against each other and determine what treatment should be followed is a matter for an experienced psychiatrist and we cannot go into further details here.

Much the same may be said of obstacles to male potency. I have already dealt at length with *premature ejaculation*. A man's partial or complete inability to achieve an erection (impotence) is almost always caused by psychological problems, in the case of men under forty, and needs psychological treatment. On the other hand, men of fifty and upwards may notice a slight decrease in their potency, and this, even when psychological causes are partly responsible for it, can be influenced in a favorable direction by a change in the manner of life and the use of hormones.

So-called perversions—sadism, masochism, fetishism, female fantasies, homosexual urges—are almost always caused by childhood interferences with normal sexual development. Therefore they should not be interpreted or condemned as if they were morally reprehensible but treated in the businesslike psychotherapeutic way they require. Many men experience such feelings only in fantasy and one may say that masturbation by married men is generally the result of perverse urges. As it always leads to estrangement from their wives, a psychotherapist should be consulted in cases where it continues within marriage.

Erotic disturbances are as obviously a matter for psychotherapists or marriage counselors as broken bones are for a surgeon. They indicate a disturbance in the relationship between husband and wife. The frigid wife does not love her husband as a man because he has failed in his spiritual and religious duty towards her. The impotent man shrinks away from real women and shuts himself off from them behind his profession or some other defiantly male activity. Bodamer has given a very impressive description of all this, ending with the words: "The pathology of modern marriage is the pathology of the modern world."

Eros by Daylight

Like every other form of Eros, Eros is not a purely individual matter during the day but part of the fellowship between the married couple. Every step I take, every person I meet, every blossoming tree I find pleasure in is not a private affair of my own but in some way affects my wife, positively or negatively, too, either adding to our marriage or breaking it apart. But for this same reason we must not use compulsion on each other; I must not tell my wife what walks to take, what persons to meet, what books to read, for if I do she will be only an extension of my own ego instead of my "Thou" acting fruitfully upon me. Every attempt to force her to conform with me takes away the duality and we become two isolated individuals.

The same is true of our failings. Every one of my wife's failings is the reflection of some failing of mine, and when I labor to get rid of my own failings I am at the same time removing my wife's. The authoritative and occasionally brutal husband generally has a wife who gives him an inferiority complex; if a wife is jealous, this does not always mean that he goes with other women but that he is generally so taken up with other things that he shows her too little affection; the barfly often has a wife who does not know how to keep him at home and the husband of the hysterical wife is almost always a bore. This list of ill-adjusted couples may be extended indefinitely. Every husband should try at least once to ask himself really seriously what failings of his own have either caused or encouraged the failings all too obvious in his wife, and every wife should ask herself the same question about her husband. If the two of them consider the matter together and pray to God about it, they generally will find astonishing things beginning to happen.

To me, only my own failings seem important and interesting, and my wife's seem largely her own concern too. A friend once told me that he had discovered that in marriage two and two make a hundred. When I asked him what on earth he meant by this he gave me the following explanation. "When I have a row with my wife I am convinced that I am ninety-eight per cent in the right and she believes the same of herself, but when we each try to remedy the remaining two per cent and apologize for it the row is a hundred per cent over." These mathematics are infallible. The little words "I'm sorry," "You're quite right," have transforming powers within marriage. But of course they only work when I use them of my own free will—not when

I at last manage to force my wife to realize her own failings and apologize for them.

Eros displays itself during the day in a hundred ways—in the way the wife dresses, or prepares and serves her husband's meals, or looks after the house and welcomes her guests; in the way the husband cares for his wife, and does the heavy work for her and delights her by little surprises, and looks after their money affairs over the years, and in general makes her feel that he is a tower of strength to her.

The important thing is to organize the day properly. Every day should have its high spots to be looked forward to—mealtimes, games, music, or reading in the evenings, and when possible a short walk together first thing in the morning, at night, or both. Morning prayers with a reading from the Bible and silent meditation and evening prayers are pillars that uphold the day and they should not be omitted under any circumstances. The week too should have its high spots, not only at the weekend but as far as possible on some special evening in between. Finally, there should be special short or long holidays over and above the traditional days, as well as tours or expeditions, festive occasions of some kind or another to mark and give variety to the passage of time.

The secret of always having enough time consists in not doing what one wants to do or thinks a good or obvious thing to do but to do what God wants and nothing else. And for that one must listen to Him and be obedient to Him.

There is another thing about the matter of time: we must not only do the right thing but do it at the right moment. For everything there is a right time and a wrong time; there are times when all goes easily and others when the going is difficult. When the husband comes home tired, the wife need not brandish the coal bill in his face and tell him that it is rent day. When the wife is feeling delighted with a new scarf or something for the house the husband need not dampen her spirits by telling her she should start economizing and buy only what is absolutely necessary. If the husband is puzzling over a difficult letter or the wife is counting the stitches in a sweater she has just started knitting, it is only to be expected that the most ardent love-making will not be amicably received. In big matters too we must do things at the right time. Time belongs to God; He alone knows its shape, and He alone can show us how to fit in with it.

Erotic fellowship is an art. Real skill in it, however, always depends on an inner attention to God. Technique is useful, but not essential. To play the violin properly a good instrument, a good bow, and some rosin are required, but the really decisive factor is the player. In marriage, the two lovers are the determinant factors, whose relationship matures as they comply with God's first commandment.

The Mastery of Sex

In contrast to this positive evaluation of Eros, there has been in all ages and all religions an idea of chastity or virginity as the highest ideal, with Eros regarded as an inferior if not an actually sinful thing. The Bible has in general a very positive attitude toward sex but even there we hear this other voice. In Matthew 19:12, for instance, Jesus speaks of "eunuchs which have made themselves eunuchs for the kingdom of heaven's sake. He that is able to receive it, let him receive it!" Paul says, in the middle of the passage about marriage, "I would that all men were even as I myself."[1] This provides a basis for the high notion of virginity firmly anchored in both Protestantism and Catholicism; the latest expression of it is the Encyclical "Sancta Virginitas." How can what I have just been saying be made to agree with this?

[1] I Cor. 7:7.

It is the more necessary to be clear on this point because a great many Christians, including numerous spiritual advisers, are in a permanent state of compromise about it: they really regard "sensual desire" as base and sinful but believe it to be necessary from a health point of view, and so they disseminate vague meaningless advice on "exercising moderation." The result is that sex goes on as before, but with a bad conscience. As someone said of the adherents of a certain sect: "Yes, they sin, but they don't enjoy it."

So first it must be said that sex is not a "lower impulse" at all. It is on the contrary man's highest impulse, the only impulse which can lead him beyond his ego to his mate and his child. It means the fulfillment of God's first command and so cannot possibly be a sin. We should accept the fact of sex with our whole being and practice it with a good conscience.

But this leads to a second point. Human sexuality does not only exist as it does in animals for procreation, but also, and far more so, for love. "The man cleaves to his wife, and they become one flesh." This change in the function of sex is comparable to what happened to the mouth, which changed from being an eating utensil to become an organ of speech, and to the hand, originally a claw to grip with, but today able to write and build and pray. Thus human sexuality comes into an ordered system; it possesses significance only within the creative order of love.

As a result of this there is the possibility of misuse, indiscipline. But it must be realized that there is lack of discipline not only in loveless pleasure seeking but also in loveless regimentation in obedience to some set of doctrinaire principles. He who "lusts after" a woman makes her into an impersonal object and therefore falls away from love; but he who constantly denigrates his sexuality tears it out of its proper context within the whole and by that very means turns it into an evil power.

But more important issues still are involved. Human sexuality is a mystery. "The anxieties suffered by modern man have arisen because we have lost the feeling of awe in face of the mystery of the sexes."[2] What makes it a mystery is the fact that not only a man and woman are involved but God too. (Thus the *taboo*—or, in Biblical terms, "the unclean," which is at the same time "the holy"—is associated with sex.) This means in practice that human sex is not a thing which works in merely natural or obvious ways but that God Himself has called it into being to help men to fulfill His purposes. We always are inclined to construct a false dilemma: either sex must dominate us, or we must dominate sex by will power. Either alternative is equally remote from the true mystery—that God wants to govern us and our sex, or rather perhaps to a very great extent governs us by means of our sex. Sexuality lived in obedience to God is chastity. As Biot says: "Man may be defined as a creature capable of chastity."

This suggests how sexuality may serve love ever more fully: First sex widens into Eros, then Eros widens into Agape—the sexual association for a specific object widens into the life association of marriage, and this in turn into an all-inclusive love and understanding of mankind. Thus, eventually it may become meaningful to forego all sexual activities in order to allow the whole power of sex to be transformed into love of God and our fellow men.

I know dozens of married couples of all ages who by voluntary agreement have renounced the sexual side of their married life and daily place their whole life force at God's disposal. Their health, happiness, and extraordinary capacity for work furnish proof that sex is not a "biological necessity," even within marriage, always provided that the renunciation comes from freedom and not from ossification or repression.

It must be added also that such self-restraint in no way

[2] Leist, p. 15.

suggests a low evaluation of Eros. On the contrary, it is only because sex is regarded as a great good that one can expect great good from sacrificing it. Anyone who is capable of surrendering this last bastion to God experiences an extraordinary feeling of freedom and is capable of breaking with every other compromise. But only when one makes the attempt does one realize how strongly one is tied to this "lawful pleasure" and how little faith one really has in absolute surrender to God. Only then can one begin to understand the real value of virginity, and how it does not mean necessarily a low estimation of the sanctity of marriage.

Let us turn to two theologians. Dietrich Bonhoeffer, a Protestant, says, "The essential element in chastity is not the renunciation of pleasure but the directing of one's whole life to one end. When this is lacking, chastity becomes ridiculous. Chastity is the prerequisite for any considered thinking."[3] The Catholic theologian August Adam insists throughout his book *Primat der Liebe* that the recognized theologians of all periods have given love precedence over chastity. "Love is not a good thing because it is chaste," he says, "but chastity is a good thing because and in so far as it is an embodiment of love. The mere rudimentary renunciation of sex is not a good thing in and of itself, and anyone who recommends it as an absolute value will arrive logically at the ideal of perfection held by Manichees and Indian fakirs." On the other hand, abstention by married persons as a sacrifice to God is one of the most effective answers to the ever increasing worship of sex which affects wide circles by its power of collective suggestion. A man who has had physical experience of how, when the living Christ wills it, this idol can fall to pieces, is in a position to proclaim a real "militant purity."

In marriage itself erotic continence usually begins by creating a crisis in which many tensions previously masked

[3] *Widerstand und Ergebung,* p. 256.

by Eros are revealed for the first time. But love can now experience a deepening process since it is its unconditional duty to make these tensions fruitful. Freedom that comes from mastering impulse permits greater frankness between parents and children, especially in the early stages. So every young couple should learn not only the art of love but the art of full self-control at least for a few months at a time.

Nothing could be more mistaken than to practice this continence as a moral requirement, or as a good work, or even from a spiritual impulse of emulation. One should remember St. Paul's warning: "Do not refuse one another except perhaps by agreement for a season, that you may devote yourselves to prayer; but then come together again, lest Satan tempt you through lack of self-control."[4] Abstention in and for itself is no better than indulgence; in fact morally it is rather inferior to it if it causes pharisaic gloom. But if it is an act of obedience to which one has been called personally by God, if the love previously regarded as the special prerogative of marriage is placed at His disposal, then it can be extraordinarily fruitful.

Speaking in general, absolute purity consists in our offering our feelings, impulses, and thoughts ever more fully to God—not so that He may remove them but that He may govern them and give us the grace to use them according to His will. But it needs very great courage to venture forth into this freedom.

Free Love

The contents of this section will hardly correspond to what the majority of readers will expect from its heading, nevertheless I appeal to them to read on. It is necessary

[4] I Cor. 7:5.

to repeat here some things that have already been said and to present them in a fresh light.

Love inside or outside marriage is not altogether free. In the first place it is limited by our egoism: we like to love and still more to be loved, but we do not wish to give ourselves to it entirely. My ambitions, plans, daily routine, favorite habits; my profession, my personal success, my friends and relatives, my hobbies and sudden crazes are some of the things I am not prepared to sacrifice for the sake of the person I marry. Even though I regard it as obvious that my wife should sacrifice such things for my sake, I will always try to wriggle out of having to give up any concrete thing myself. "You may ask anything else of me, but I won't give up my bowling!" Or, "You know I am wholly yours, but you mustn't stop me making myself attractive to other men!" It does not matter whether we are actually in the right or not; here the only thing to realize is that some things are more important than love to us and keep our love from being free.

Love is still more limited by lust. (This applies particularly to me.) If a husband lusts after his wife he imagines that he loves her passionately, but if for any reason the wife refuses to give herself to him this love comes to an end with remarkable promptitude and very bitter words can be said. What is still more remarkable is that men who get full sexual satisfaction from their wives may still keep eying other women, and often a short absence from home or some other chance occasion is enough to start him running after another woman. Such men explain that they are made in such a way that they can be in love with several women at the same time. The fact is that their lust is orientated (as it always is) towards women in general, and so they cannot really love any individual woman properly— not even their own wife. Finally love can fail to be free, paradoxically, because husband and wife are tied to each other. They have eyes for each other, and nothing else in heaven or on earth. The result is that they always are giving in to each other: there are two slaves and no master. Each feels the burden of the other's welfare in the shape of worry, meaningless worry: so the husband "for his own good" is forbidden to ski or swim or travel or go out at night, and is stuffed with vitamins and coffee, and to avoid any risks of upset the couple confine themselves to two children. *Egoïsme à deux* becomes *égoïsme au carré*. Genuine love creates a duality, but when there is only bondage both sides are self-centered and alone—one and one do not in this case make two.

True love, on the other hand, sets each partner free.

The truly married have no secrets from each other, for they trust each other and know that all their problems, even their own sins and failures, will be solved better with the help of the other than alone. The two are as clear as crystal to each other.

The truly married try to distinguish love from lust: I love the other for his own sake, and that leads to pleasure for me; whereas I lust after him to satisfy the demands of my own egoism. The pleasure true love bestows is fresh, unexpected, overpowering every time; whereas the pleasure of lust comes as expected—it is an old record that has been played many times before. Lustful looks at other women and fantasies and other images are records of this kind.

The truly married are resolved once and for all to give up their own wills. It is very simple: every time I am irritated by my wife, every time I feel misunderstood and suffer from a feeling of self-pity, every time I am hasty and think I know better, every time I want to "make her happy" against her will, then my own unbridled egoism is asserting itself and gaining temporary control over my love. These symptoms will keep appearing whenever my will is crossed—until it has been crossed out.

The truly married love each other in a way that leaves them free for the love of God. They no longer belong to each other but belong together to God and together obey His voice.

When two human beings love each other they listen to each other. When we love God we listen to Him, beginning each day by being quiet and reading His word and trying to hear what He has to say to us personally. True freedom consists in doing the will of God and not the will of man or our own selfish will. Love gives us this freedom. Of course we fail again and again. But if we take God's will absolutely seriously then we are able to realize how great our own failures are and forgive our partner for hers. Thus husband and wife remind each other of the Absolute and pronounce forgiveness to each other. This is their "priestly" service to each other. As Luther says, "We ought to be Christs to one another."

In a union such as this, sex is still part of the secret which unites husband and wife but it is no longer the final goal. Mere carnal love has been discarded in preference to a more mature love which encompasses the entire being of the marriage partner. For this reason husband and wife are able to extend their fellowship to include single men or women and be of help and support to them in their difficulties without causing jealousy to anyone. All true love, in marriage or celibacy, is the gift of God.

4.

THE FRUIT OF MARRIAGE

Most human beings feel the urge towards the other sex without thinking of propagation, and nurse a desire for children without feeling any sexual inclinations. Many primitive peoples are unaware of the connection between sexual intercourse and propagation, and there are girls who want a child but not a man.

This does not alter the fact that sexual union and propagation are intimately involved. A young couple have no need to ask, "Do we want children or not? When shall we have them? How many shall we have?" They will accept children as a blessing as a matter of course, as and when they arrive. This is something we cannot decide by our own "desires and inclinations"; we are under an order entirely transcending us. Helene Deutsch accepts these ideas as findings based on psychological experience and says, "Coitus is the beginning of a process that reaches it climax in birth."

Heredity

When children are mentioned, we at once think of them as carrying over into the next generation qualities inherited from us. As a great deal of confusion still prevails on this subject I must mention the essential facts.

Putting it all very approximately, we may say that inherited qualities like eye color, shape of nose, blood group, a musical ear, or a tendency to some disease, all derive from minute granules in the heart of the ovum or seed cell. These single granules containing the hereditary factors—"genes" as they are called—are found in "chromosomes," the central meshes of the seminal cell, like pearls on a string. At conception the male and female chromosomes come up against each other and the separate genes combine. Then either of the two following possibilities may occur: a certain characteristic in the child may come from a blending of the characteristics of both parents (father of blood group A, mother blood group B, child AB) or else— and this happens much more frequently—one inherited tendency will outweigh the other and apparently make it vanish (blue-eyed father, brown-eyed mother, brown-eyed child). The hereditary characteristic that wins this contest is called the "dominant," the loser is the "recessive."

This last point is particularly important in understanding how the science of heredity works in practice, for recessive qualities that have apparently vanished in some particular individual can suddenly appear in his children, provided that they do not encounter another contrary tendency and above all do not come up against a similar recessive tendency in the partner. This explains why some hereditary talent or disease may "jump" one or two generations and pop up fifty years later as an apparently new attribute. A man need not himself have suffered from a disease in order to transmit a hereditary tendency to it.

But the boundary between inheritable and non-inheritable diseases is not absolutely fixed. There are pure inherited diseases, independent of any external influences, and there are diseases like measles which are occasioned quite externally and attack anyone infected by them quite independently of inherited tendencies. Most diseases come somewhere between these two extremes. Epilepsy is based on a hereditary tendency but may first develop through a brain disturbance or an infection; tuberculosis is infectious, but hereditary tendencies determine which organ it attacks.

Among the serious diseases which are entirely or almost entirely due to a hereditary tendency are congenital imbecility, schizophrenia, manic-depressive insanity, certain forms of epilepsy, congenital deaf-and-dumbness, certain forms of blindness, diabetes and clubfeet, anemia and a whole range of rarer diseases. Particularly important, again, is the rather vague group of "psychopaths" to which most alcoholics, vagabonds, and criminals belong. These troubles usually are dismissed as "peculiarities," "originality," "individual oddities," and it is far too little realized that they are genuine inherited diseases, especially when a large number of elements come together in one person. On the other hand acquired diseases such as infantile paralysis, Parkinson's disease, and as a rule cancer are not inherited directly although the tendency toward these diseases may be inherited.

For a concrete picture of the dangers involved in heredity it should be noticed that out of every hundred children whose fathers or mothers are or have been schizophrenic, for example (the hereditary danger exists independently of any temporary cure of the carrier of the disease) an average of sixteen suffer from schizophrenia too and thirty-three become psychopaths. So a schizophrenic has one chance in two of having mentally diseased children. If both parents are schizophrenic, sixty-four per cent of the children suffer from schizophrenia and thirty-two per cent become psychopathic. Almost all are therefore abnormal. If on the other hand one of the grandparents is diseased, while the parents are healthy, the number of schizophrenic and psychopathic grandchildren sinks to three per cent and fourteen per cent respectively, while the percentage for nephews and cousins is less than two per cent and five per cent and is therefore no higher than the average figure for the total population. One may say therefore that in practice people who suffer or have suffered from a serious inherited disease should not have children, nor should people among whose *near relatives* such diseases are common. If, however, there has only been a single case of the illness of a distant relative it usually will be safe to have children provided the person one marries is unaffected. In all doubtful cases an experienced physician should be consulted and given as full as possible genealogical trees of the two families, showing the healthy members along with the rest.

The tendency today is to attribute as much importance to early upbringing as to heredity. Lack of affection and security, particularly from the mother, can lead to a feeling of abandonment which may affect a child for the rest of its life, while a loving and sensible upbringing—no "spoiling"—can sometimes overcome even a deeply ingrained hereditary tendency by dealing with it positively instead of allowing it to take the shape of a disease. This does not mean that one can afford to neglect or disregard hereditary tendencies but that one should recognize what is possible in these situations. Childlessness may be one of these possibilities.

Questions are asked frequently in this connection as to what is meant by the "Rhesus Factor"—"Rh." About sixteen per cent of people are "rhesus-negative" (Rh—) and eighty-four per cent "rhesus-positive" (Rh+). When a Rh— woman is expecting a child by a Rh+ man it may be Rh+ like its father or Rh— like its mother. In some cases some of the Rh+ blood may get into the mother's veins and produce "antibodies" in her—i.e. a defensive substance which possesses the power to disintegrate Rh+ blood. In this case the mother is "sensitized" against Rh+. If this sensitized mother now has a second child which is Rh+ like the first the mother's antibodies may disintegrate its blood so that either before or during birth it contracts a severe attack of jaundice that destroys the red blood corpuscles (this is not to be confused with the jaundice normal to newborn children) and may even kill it. Nowadays this jaundice can generally be cured by an immediate blood transfusion. It is clear, then, that the Rh factor can have harmful results only when (a) a Rh— woman becomes pregnant by a Rh+ man (not vice versa), (b) when former children have similarly been Rh+, and (c) when the mother has been sensitized by them. In the large majority of marriages between Rh— women and Rh+ men—there are millions of them—nothing happens; but when a number of unfavorable conditions come together the result of course may be serious. Owing to the low proportion of such mischances one cannot on principle advise a Rh— girl not to marry a Rh+ man. If, however, a sensitized Rh— mother loses one child through jaundice there is a great probability that the same thing will happen to the next unless it receives a blood transfusion as soon as it is born. But even here a complete cure is quite likely.

"Expecting"

There is hardly any human responsibility greater than that of the mother who carries her child within her for nine whole months. This responsibility is shared by the father, since the mother's behavior and attitude depend to a large extent on his.

Pregnancy is not a disease, and the expectant mother should make as little change as possible in her manner of life. During the first few months the embryo is still not anchored firmly enough to prevent the possibility of a miscarriage should she receive a severe shake such as may come from jumping or riding or traveling in a jolty vehicle, or suffer some psychological disturbance or catch an infectious disease; so women need to exercise caution during this period. The remedies for the morning sickness which occurs during these first months are various and a physician should be consulted. An unconscious defensive reaction against the child, or against the husband, or against being a woman may sometimes be a contributory cause of this trouble. But even when a young mother-to-be suffers severely at this time, she can console herself with the thought that the discomfort almost always vanishes during the fourth month and often gives place to a remarkable feeling of well-being. It should be realized that poisons like alcohol, consumed in large quantities, have a harmful effect on the child, so an expectant mother should always practice temperance. And she should make sure of sufficient exercise and fresh air.

Sexual intercourse may be continued during pregnancy without any precautions but should be given up for the last month or so before birth and after to prevent any bacteria from penetrating into the womb and possibly producing puerperal fever later on.

Psychologically speaking, many women feel particularly happy during pregnancy, while others get touchy and are easily depressed. So at this period the young husband should take special care to give his wife gallant support, understanding, and a feeling of security. This is not always easy, since during the last few months the wife is somewhat distorted physically and is psychologically more easily irritated than usual. He should control himself sexually during this period. This is a chance if ever there was one for him to sublimate his sex into Eros and Agape and prove himself capable of unselfish love. It is at just this time that many a woman loses her respect and therefore her love for her husband. The wife for her part should realize that her husband is often under a strain and should not neglect herself or let herself go. And when the child arrives she should not make her husband take a back seat and focus all her affection and attention on the new arrival. The husband who, rightly or wrongly, thinks himself neglected can become jealous of his child—extraordinary as it may sound—and try to take his revenge by being unfaithful to his wife. A sensible wife will do all she can to draw her husband into her maternal joys. An extremely virile man once said that during and immediately after the birth it is possible to arouse in every man a motherly vein which will bring him profound happiness. He can be not only fatherly but motherly too—first towards his wife and then towards the child. It is not unmanly for a man to act as assistant nurse to his wife, to bathe the baby and put its diaper on—just as the maternal affection newly felt by the wife does not put an end to her erotic relationship with her husband but is its proper fulfillment.

Worry about the coming event oppresses many a young wife. It should be realized that both mind and body are ripening for it and will be ready for it when it comes. Contentment and confidence are the best foundation for an easy delivery. Recently the pains have been reduced by a special breathing technique at the birth. This period may be critical: it is at this time that primitive tribes make special efforts to drive away evil spirits, and the idea has something in it. But the crisis can bind husband and wife into a unity as nothing else can, once they realize that jointly they are furthering God's work of creation.

Childlessness

When no children result in spite of normal intercourse there can be various causes. An obvious cause may be an obstruction of the seminal duct or tubes in husband or wife as a result of inflammation. In the case of the woman the ovary may be sealed up only slightly and can be freed by a slight operation which involves blowing through a tube.

Childlessness may be due also to general influences like digestive troubles, lack of vitamins, infantilism, etc. The wife's psychological condition also affects her ability to conceive. Orgasm is not absolutely necessary—many frigid women become mothers—but it seems to encourage conception.

There are also men and women individually potent enough who for some special reason are incapable of having children together. The choice of the day of conception is of particular importance, and I shall be dealing with this matter in the next section.

Treatment for childlessness requires an accurate examination of the wife, and also of the husband, or at least a microscopic investigation of his seed, because the source of the trouble is as often as not to be found in the husband. In any case the wife's psychological attitude to her husband and having a child has to be taken into consideration. There are doctors who specialize in the treatment of childlessness and it is worth exploring this matter thoroughly.

If the cause is found in the husband, and he and his wife are eager for a child, then artificial insemination may be tried. When possible the husband's semen is used, but if he is unable to produce any living sperm the semen of some other man who neither knows nor is known by the wife is used instead. Three or four, sometimes more, injections are required. In a majority of cases pregnancies have resulted, and Joel gives some examples of happy effects on inconsolable couples. I myself know of only one case, and it was successful. Nonetheless there are many weighty objections, both ethical and psychological, to this procedure, for no one quite knows what he is doing when he introduces an extraneous element into marriage in this way. The Roman Catholic Church forbids all artificial insemination, while the Church of England only allows it with the husband's semen. So far the Protestant Church generally has not expressed any attitude, but no Protestant theologian has declared himself to be in favor of artificial insemination from an outside source. Anyone who has a paramount wish to have a child can adopt one; and such a course is very much preferable.

Only after every means has been tried and found useless should a couple resign themselves to the fact of childlessness. It is possible for childless couples to adopt orphans and thus help to remove great misery. They also can dedicate themselves to some task, social, cultural, or religious, and thus develop a unique intellectual fellowship. I know many childless married couples who have attained to real fullness of living by one or other of these means.

Birth Control

During the last thirty years few questions have been as passionately discussed as the rights and wrongs of deliberately limiting the number of children in a marriage. I will give you a short outline of the problem, since it is impossible to cover all the arguments for and against.

That the problem is now more acute than it ever was in the past is due to the following causes:

Decrease of infant mortality: in the U.S. in 1964 one child in fifty died; in 1875 one in five; before that one in two. In ninety-three years infant mortality has been reduced to one-tenth of what it was.

A higher valuation of the life of the mother: Deaths as the result of birth or illness caused by birth used to be much more frequent than they are now.

Changes in social structure: For a farmer or craftsman children meant helping hands before very long, but for factory workers and employees they are economically a liability.

Higher educational demands: Children require a much

greater amount of time, energy, and money from their parents than they used to.

The increased importance of intellectual companionship in marriage: This, if only in games, plays a much greater part today than it used to, and it takes a proportionate amount of time and energy from the wife's attention to her purely maternal functions.

In the case of the lower income groups these factors have now combined with the elementary struggle for existence and above all with the housing shortage. In the middle class these factors have combined with fears of sinking into the proletariat, and in the remaining classes with greater demands from life generally. One may or may not regret this, but a houseful of children no longer has the same ideological significance as it had in Old Testament times.

Above all, the dynamics of the world's population have changed. Improved sanitary conditions have led to rapid population growth. It took 230 years, between 1600 and 1830, for the world's population to double. It doubled again in the next one hundred years. Now it takes only thirty-nine years for the world's population to double, and it is estimated that in the year 2000 there will be four times as many people in the world as there were in 1900. According to United Nations statistics, the world's population was increasing every day between mid-1965 and mid-1966 by 167,000 people.

The population explosion is especially noticeable in the developing countries where the mortality rate has been cut drastically while the birth rate frequently continues on a level as high as 40 or even 60 per 1000 inhabitants. (In Europe the rate is nineteen.)

All this makes appropriate and responsible birth control a necessity of the times, especially in developing countries. Birth control is the natural answer to the prolongation of man's life. (In India the average life span has grown from twenty-seven years in 1948 to forty-eight years in 1965 and is expected to reach sixty years by 1970.)

What, then, is the ethical-theological view of birth control? If one were to summarize briefly the debate that has been going on for several decades among such theologians as Emil Brunner, Karl Barth, and Roger Muhl among the Protestants, and Herbert Doms, Jakob David, Franz Böckle, Edward Schillebeeckx, and Georg Scherer among the Roman Catholics, one would come up with the following formulation: Marriage is a complete union of two persons which is meaningful in itself. Procreation, as well as love, is a gift of grace entailing sacred duty. The will to have children is therefore incumbent in every marriage and only the most serious considerations should be allowed to change this basic attitude. Where such reasons exist, the couple should choose the method of birth control that would "best convey the tenderness that should be expressed in the act of surrender" (Böckle).

For a long time it was believed that the "nature" of the sex act would be spoiled by any attempt to prevent procreation. The aforementioned theologians, however, hold that the human act should not be evaluated from a purely biological viewpoint, but, rather, as a human, personal act (actus humanus) deeply anchored in the marriage and always—even when, for serious reasons, procreation must be avoided—expressing the love between man and woman.

Admittedly, the discussion among Roman Catholics hasn't been closed yet. In the "Pastoral Constitution" of the Vatican Council we find the statement: "In their duty to procreate and to bring up children, which is to be considered their unique calling, the partners of a marriage recognize themselves as collaborators of God the Creator and interpreters of His love. Therefore, they will fulfill their duty with human and Christian responsibility and seek the right decisions in the light of divine counsel. They will consider their own well-being as well as that of their children—those born as well as those not yet born. They will consider the material and the spiritual conditions of the times and their own personal conditions and be responsible towards the world and the Church. The final decision must be their own. . . . The marriage, however, has not been instituted for the sole purpose of procreation, but also to enhance a unique and indivisible personal togetherness and to further the well-being of their children. . . ." (Chapter 50.)

This indicates that the majority of the Council's commission on birth control favored a liberal approach wherever the reasons for such control were of a serious nature. It is, however, still not certain that their views will ultimately prevail.

On the practical level, the question facing a married couple is not that of arbitrary decisions on whether or not to have children. Rather, it should be a matter of seeking in every individual instance the course that will have God's approval. Since we find ourselves in a world in which the income of the father of a large family is hardly larger than that of an unmarried man, and since many other adverse conditions may have to be taken into account, such as sickness or detrimental hereditary tendencies, we must try to determine what God requires of us under such circumstances. How many children will He give His blessing to, and what course of action does He indicate after that number has been reached? No one can take this decision away from us, or assume our responsibility for it for us. But usually it will be advisable to seek the advice of a trustworthy third party on this question of birth regulation, to be sure of avoiding both anxious scruples and also comfortable egoism.

The Church of Neuchâtel manifesto on marriage says: "You are responsible for the powers and means which God has entrusted you with for the upbringing of your children; so you are also responsible for their number. Be on your guard against limiting this number out of anxiety, sloth or selfishness, and also against thoughtlessly letting it increase.

There are times when a married couple, out of regard for the health of the mother or the good of the children, will avoid conception without giving up conjugal relations: they will not deny themselves to each other, but think of the words of St. Paul, 'For the wife does not rule over her own body, but the husband does; likewise the husband does not rule over his own body, but the wife does.' "

For Protestants and Catholics alike it is not the method of contraception that makes it "good" or "bad" but the attitude and motive behind it. It is not a case of an absolute, self-centered freedom, but a freedom within God's order, the freedom of obedience. This order is defined in one way by Roman Catholics and in another way by Protestants. One defines it chiefly in terms of nature, the other in terms of responsibility. But both employ these terms in a subordinate sense and we should not be misled and fail to see the fundamental unity of viewpoint behind them.

Moreover one can form a very positive understanding of the term "birth control." "When ventured upon in faith it may signify a conscious intentional renunciation of the possibility of renunciation, a joyfulness and a willingness to have children and be a parent."[1] Responsible parenthood, in fact!

Having thus tried to reach clarity on the fundamentals, I shall in the following pages try to give a purely technical account of the methods which can be employed to secure contraception.

1) Complete abstention may in some very special instances be the right answer to a couple's problems—at least for a while. But if it is employed *solely* for the sake of contraception it almost always leads to inner complications, psychological damage, and the mutual alienation of wife and husband. Morally it is no "better" than any other method.

[1] *Ibid.*, p. 305.

2) Periodical abstention, often called the "Rhythm Method," based on the work of Knaus and Ogino, is rooted in their findings that normally conception takes place when the ovum separates itself from the ovary. According to Knaus this occurs on the fifteenth day before the next period (though this has been questioned). When the period recurs regularly every twenty-eight days, therefore, the thirteenth day from the beginning of the last period will probably be the first day of conception. If one then remembers that spermatozoa remain capable of germinating for thirty-six hours, one must, to be safe, insert a few days before and after this thirteenth day and, therefore, give up intercourse from the tenth to the seventeenth day after the beginning of the period. But the period very rarely occurs as regularly as this, and these calculations all depend on when the next period begins. One, therefore, needs to know the amount of variation, before one can estimate when it will most probably occur. This makes it necessary to keep an accurate record over at least a year of the date when each period begins and then it will be possible to calculate the longest and the shortest intervals. The following rule can then be applied: Subtract nineteen from the shortest menstrual month in the list of variations and you will have the latest day that is definitely sterile. After that, subtract ten from the longest menstrual month on your list of variations and you will have the earliest day that is definitely sterile before the next period. This rule, which is more cautious than Knaus's, can be regarded as infallible provided the calculations are correct and the limits strictly adhered to. Suspicions are warranted by the following considerations: exceptional variations of a week or more can occur, making all calculation vain; in certain women orgasm seems to release the ovum with the result that conception takes place despite any previous calculations; after birth conception can take place before recurrence of the period, so that one has no fixed point from which to make any calculations. It also must be regarded

as a disadvantage that many women feel their strongest erotic desires when they are most ready to conceive and it is unnatural for them to abstain then. Periodical abstention may have great advantages, but it is not infallible—van de Velde has made observations which show that conception can take place on every day of the month—and when the period recurs at irregular intervals an unreasonably long period of continence is required.

The calculations here given for the purpose of avoiding conception may be given a positive application in cases of apparent sterility: sexual intercourse should then take place especially during the days immediately following the release of the ovum.

3) Variations in the wife's temperature graph supply a safer guide to the day when the ovum is released. If the temperature is taken each morning at the same hour it will be found to remain more or less constant from the first day of the period until the day the ovum is released, between 97° and 98° (depending upon the individual), and that just before this day it rises, suddenly or gradually, by about ½–1 degree and remains there until shortly before the start of the next period. The greatest readiness to conceive occurs on the day of the rise in temperature, while after the second day at this high temperature a fairly assured period of sterility sets in. This method allows a shortening of the period of abstention by a few days and makes it possible to recognize the onset of pregnancy by the fact that the temperature continues to be high. But here also of course there are individual variations and peculiarities. For measuring the temperature any good fever thermometer will suffice; there is no need whatsoever to employ expensive instruments like the ones used by specialists.

It is advisable for young couples first to try abstention (methods 2 and 3) to familiarize themselves with the special rhythms. This will enable them to space births out according to their desires and to avoid situations when avoidance of pregnancy becomes a necessity. In general, it is much less taxing for a mother to bear six children between the ages of twenty-two and thirty-four than to bear four children between twenty-two and twenty-six.

4) *Carezza-praxis* (coitus reservatus) consists in making intercourse last as long as possible without allowing ejaculation to take place. This means climbing to a high plateau without attaining to one's own summit. Opinions about it differ greatly. Apart from the difficulty the husband has in suppressing his own orgasm, various authorities, van de Velde for instance, issue warnings against it, but without giving any reasons. Chesser, Stopes, etc. admit its practicability provided the necessary practice has been done.

5) In *interrupted intercourse* (coitus interruptus or copula diminuata), the husband withdraws immediately before ejaculation. If he can make the union last until the wife has had her orgasm and is not himself too sensitive there is not much to be said against the practice from a medical point of view. But apart from this the time is usually too short, of course, for the wife to experience any pleasure—not to speak of her continual fears that the husband will not withdraw in time. So one must as a rule advise against this type of contraceptive as having no advantages, psychological, aesthetic, or moral.

6) The *condom* or *contraceptive* is a sort of rubber article like the finger of a glove which can be pulled over the erect penis before intercourse. It is—provided it does not get torn—the safest means of contraception. The disadvantages are that it must be put on during love-play, which may prove psychologically upsetting. Also, the wife feels no sensation as a result of the outpouring of the semen, which may lead to a feeling of disappointment. Finally, when this method is employed, it is impossible for

the fluid accompanying the sperm to be absorbed through the walls of the vagina, which according to certain authorities assures the wife of having the right supply of hormones. The "American tips" are smaller condoms covering only the head of the penis.

7) *Rings, diaphragms or occlusive pessaries* for women have the advantage of staying in place for a considerable time and do not require any attention immediately before or after intercourse. Women can insert them themselves but a doctor's advice is desirable to help in choosing the right size and fit to begin with. The occlusive pessary does not offer much security except in combination with some sperm-killing ointment.

8) *Cervical caps, portio-caps, cervix-occlusive pessaries* of metal or plastic must be inserted by a physician every time, but can in theory at least stay in place from one period to another. But they may easily cause serious inflammation of the mucous membrane and therefore are not often employed nowadays.

9) *Chemical contraceptives* in the form of capsules, pills, or ointments, inserted into the vagina shortly before intercourse, have none of them proved infallible so far, nor has it been established that, in spite of the employment of the chemical preventative, when a child is born it does not suffer injury from it. If this method is used, it is strongly recommended for this expedient to be *combined* with a condom or a diaphragm to make it safer.

10) The Intrauterine-Contraceptive Device (IUCD or IUD) is a plastic bow or spiral placed in the womb for an indefinite period. This device is quite widely used in America even though most European doctors remain hesitant about its use. Apparently, the device does not prevent fertilization of the ovum but keeps it from nesting in the

wall of the womb. With a little sophistry, this can be described as very early abortion. Its durability makes the use of this device so simple that, at least for the time being, it is considered most appropriate for birth control in underdeveloped countries.

11) The hormonal-ovulation preventer, commonly known as "The Pill," is the most popular and, if properly used, the safest birth-control device known today. It's easy because it's taken orally. Usually, a combination of pills of estrogen and progesteron are taken for periods of twenty to twenty-two days. Sensitive women may experience nausea similar to that in early stages of pregnancy. Also, the cessation of menstrual cycles may cause feelings of spiritual deprivation. Finally, it is possible that a woman's eroticism may diminish. However, the newest method permits the taking primarily of estrogen for fifteen days and then the combination pill for five days. This so-called "sequence method" is less likely to cause nausea and, above all, libido disturbances.

Obviously choosing a contraceptive is not an altogether simple matter and a doctor should always be consulted, once the decision has been made to use some method of contraception. There is no method which is the best in all conceivable circumstances and methods must be adapted to suit individual cases.

Sterilization, i.e. the application of a ligature to the tubes in the case of the woman and to the seminal duct in the case of the man, should only be contemplated after very careful consideration indeed. The Roman Catholic Church condemns it absolutely. If it seems to be necessary, it should still never be resorted to by people under thirty and with less than three children. It should be realized that —unlike the case of castration—nothing is removed: the sensations remain exactly the same after the operation as before. The person concerned must be known to desire of his own free will to have the operation performed and must have had it accurately explained to him. It also should be realized that, technically speaking, it is much easier to carry it out on the husband than on the wife, so in all cases where the husband is diseased or where reasons affecting both, e.g. economic ones, drive them to have recourse to it, it should be performed not on the wife but on the husband. But it always involves a hard and usually irrevocable decision and it should never be considered except as a last resort: doctors who recommend sterilization as a matter of course after the birth of the second or third child are guilty of most improper conduct.

When sterilization has been performed on the woman, it can theoretically be counteracted by a second operation but in practice this is very doubtful.

I prefer not to say anything about *abortion,* which is never a method of regulating births but always, even in the very earliest stages, the slaughter of a small human being, a thing which can never be "permissible" and can at best be the lesser of two evils, when the mother's life is directly threatened by a prolongation of her pregnancy.

I must end with a solemn word of warning. We must often be thankful for contraceptives, but the great danger in using these technical things lies in the failure to realize the inherent problem—in other words, using them quite arbitrarily and ignoring the profound association God has once and for all established between sexual union and procreation.

At times it may be the right response to a personal duty imposed by God to get these two things apart, but we must always remember the other possibility, continence. Perhaps having to give up having children may be a sign that we are to rise to a new type of love. Every time a contraceptive is used, one should ask oneself why.

Modern man's willfulness and technical arrogance are just as dangerous as moral rigidity and cheap compromises that stultify all spiritual values. The more unconditionally we love God, the more surely He will lead us either to have children, or to prevention, or to abstention; and He will give us the strength and joy to follow His way.

Managing a Family

The moment a child comes on the scene the marriage becomes a family. Husband and wife become father and mother, and a new sort of hierarchy comes into being. I cannot go into the problem of the upbringing of children here, but I should like to try to state one fundamental principle.

Husband and wife are "one flesh." This never applies to parents and children. It is the other way round. The child *was* part of its mother's body, but in baptism—or circumcision as the case may be—it comes before God as an independent person. In virtue of this it no longer belongs to the parents but to God. This of course does not exhaust the meaning of baptism, but it does perhaps show a side of it which might serve to justify infant baptism.

Even though at times the bonds of feeling between mother and child are closer than those between husband and wife, this must not be allowed to obscure the divine ordinance by which husband and wife become one flesh whereas the child is born from the mother's body and becomes an independent human being. This lies behind the parents' solidarity as against the child, which is absolute and not to be denied in any circumstances. Anyone who ridicules husband and wife before a child or complains about them to it is not only attacking a marriage, but also, as far as the child is concerned, the sacred ordinance of the family.

One of the most tragic features of the world we live in is the way women increasingly evade their role of motherhood and men even more evade their role as fathers.

Women who are intellectually cultured or professionally active often feel it beneath their dignity to be mothers. When they can, they go on with their professions, handing the children over to servants. They do irreparable harm to their children, and leave their most difficult, most demanding, most sacred duty undone—the duty of bringing their children up properly.

We live in a one-sidedly masculine world, but fathers are nevertheless lacking in it. A man who becomes a father receives his office from the hand of God. "The highest form of manhood means realizing and achieving one's religious destiny as a husband. This alone makes a man fit and able to be the representative, however imperfect, of God Himself."[2]

Father and mother give each other security; and when one of them fails the other suffers for it. Where security is wanting, anxiety takes its place, and mankind takes flight into some kind of mania. That is a fair picture of our own day, and the only cure for it is—real fathers and mothers.

[2] Bodamer, p. 88.

5.

HEARTH AND HOME

"All you need for marriage is—a man, a woman, a few children, a few things to eat with and sleep on, and maybe an animal or two. It is like the beginning of creation. And from the beginning of creation to the present day that is what it has always been—a man and a woman with a few things and a few animals in the marriage house. Fortunes have been made and lost, masses of human beings have covered the face of the earth and vanished under it, there has been a Flood and a new earth, and always there has been this man and woman standing side by side with their children and a few things in the marriage house—the place one can return to again and again, the place one can set out from, again and again. . . . In the world outside, men take their existence for granted, like something ready-made, but in the marriage house there is one man and one woman, with a few children and a few things: existence is at its beginning, and the thrill of existence too—and the man feels this to be so, feels the sense of awe and danger at something happening for the very first time. . . . Here in the marriage house things are primitive again and take on the beautiful insecurity of the primitive. A wooden floor is laid in a house that they have built themselves, and it seems to them that for the first time they are cutting themselves off from direct contact with the earth—they look a little anxiously at the floor, there is wood between the soles of their feet and the earth; they are a little further away from the earth but nearer to each other. . . . Or they plant a tree in their garden. It is as if it were the very first time that a man and woman had planted a tree together; they are astonished that the earth holds it up and that the weight of heaven does not weigh it down. And when in autumn the fruit hangs heavy upon its boughs as if to weigh it down to the earth from which it came, and when the sound of fruit falling in other men's fields strikes their ears—as if the sound of falling fruit were one tree's answer to another, as cocks answer one another across the emptiness of the morning—then, when they see that their tree is not unique but bears red apples like the trees of other men, they are not disappointed but happy that their tree, the tree belonging to their marriage house, is a part of a whole order of trees. Nor do they feel this order to be a mechanical thing; it seems to them to have been made especially for them, and created for the first time."

The above words by Max Picard portray in a way not to be surpassed the eternal form marriage takes, not only as a psychological relationship between husband and wife but as something on which the whole of human society depends.

Under the influence of modern psychology marriage has been all too glibly identified with love, so that a marriage where love has for the time being grown weak is declared to be "pointless" and a grand passion which refuses nevertheless to bind itself is without further examination given the title of "free love." Against this it must be said again and again that while marriage generally (not always) arises as a result of love, and under favorable conditions is also nourished by love, it still forms an independent organism transcending love. Love is to marriage what sap is to a tree: out of it grow stem, leaves, and fruit, which last on even when the sap ceases to flow in winter. Indeed these things, once grown, cause a fresh flow of sap.

The fruit of marriage is the child. Along with the parents it forms the living community of the family. To the family belong too all the ideas associated with the hearth around which the family gather and at which outsiders are allowed to sit. This does not necessarily mean comfortable middle-class homes: the "hearth" may be a wood fire under the open sky or a small stove in the corner of a bedroom; the essential point is that here individual human beings are naturally united without any other condition than that of being alive, and as a result of this can face the world together and can agree to welcome the outsider into their midst. The family is to the individual what surface is to line: it is an "area" which has room for many things; it is a "yard" for men and beasts, a womb in which life is secure and can mature.

The Wedding

Everywhere and at all times marriage has been celebrated by a ceremonial act, a wedding. Marriage is not a private affair between a man and a maid but in some way a concern of the whole community: the names must be publicly posted for ten days, the ceremony must take place before two witnesses in a place accessible to the public, it is heralded by church bells and sealed by a splendid feast—the "wedding breakfast."

Even in primitive times the marriage rites recognized the three essential elements in marriage:

1) leaving father and mother—detaching oneself clearly and irrevocably from the family to which one has hitherto belonged;

2) cleaving to wife or husband—breaking the bonds with one's parents because of love of one's mate and taking such action as will permit this love to mature;

3) becoming one flesh—bodily union, community of goods, the child in common.

These three things still make up marriage today, and it is important to give each of them their due and to realize that no one of them can be neglected if there is to be a true marriage.

There is a tendency today to regard the wedding ceremony as a mere external convention. Marriage, people say, is primarily an emotional attachment between two young human beings—frequently consummated on the quiet, with nothing left to be done but the mere formality of informing their friends and relations of the fact. I once shared this view myself but I have now come to regard it as hopelessly wrong. A marriage based on feeling alone vanishes with the feeling and then it seems mere hypocrisy to those concerned not to be allowed to divorce each other. The purely external registration or "blessing" of an already consummated marriage takes away the real significance and irrevocable character of the setting up of hearth and home.

The marriage service of the Church of England, in which the vows of wedlock and betrothal are first proclaimed by the minister and then repeated word for word by husband and wife, is extraordinarily impressive, and makes both the newly married couple and the whole congregation feel that something is taking place which entirely transcends their own personal will and sphere.

Incipit vita nova ("Here begins a new life") should be the motto for every wedding day—in a personal sense, and as regards the relationship to the two families (I have dealt with this in Chapter 1) and also as regards the relationship with the outside world, which husband and wife henceforth will face as a unity. "Whither thou goest, I will go; and where thou lodgest, I will lodge: thy people shall be my people, and thy God my God. Where thou diest, will I die, and there will I be buried."[1]

Subordination

Within the family group each member plays a distinctive part, combining the best service to the whole with the best sort of self-development. In this sense a sacred order—a "hierarchy"—governs the family: the husband is its "head," the wife its "heart," as is evident from the parts they have to play as father and mother. It is not a good thing for these parts to be changed, for the wife to be the stronger one and the husband the more sensitive, for apart from the upsets described in Chapter 2 this gives the children a false idea of the ideals at which they should aim. The daughters develop a hard masculine manner and a faintly patronizing air towards the opposite sex, while the sons suffer from a vain longing for true warmth of feeling, cultivate a private emotional life of their own, and often marry rather haughty, frigid women on whom they first project all their love and then become disillusioned—or else they become misogynists and in certain circumstances develop homosexual leanings.

Nevertheless, as Ernst Michel and Eugen Rosenstock have shown, the parts played by husband and wife both oscillate between two poles. The married man who "possesses" his wife ought also to be a wooer and go on courting her, and the mother should go on being her husband's bride and beloved. "Woe to the mother who insists on being nothing but a mother, and to the beloved who insists on being solely the beloved! Both destroy the tension sex

[1] Ruth 1:16, 17.

has created in them for the sake of real life. They are threatened by degeneration and one-sided development."

Children's independence of their parents varies according to their age. We should always remember that the goal when raising children is not to secure complete obedience from them, a sort of squad drill, but to make them able to accept the full responsibility of freedom. When a child reaches late adolescence he should be able to make his own decisions as a creature responsible to God alone and at most ask his parents for advice and be at liberty not to follow it. As regards the small child, the parents are God's representatives on earth to it—the mother representing the God of Love, the father the God of Justice. Later they become representatives of all human authority—which generally speaking is to be obeyed but can be questioned if need be, for it is not infallible. Often the parents are the child's first "enemies," and it is important for him to learn through them how to stand up to his enemies bravely and eventually come to love them.

Amongst each other, the children learn the meaning of comradeship. The eldest finds it difficult to accept the others at first, especially the second one. It should be realized that it is quite normal for jealousy to provoke unconscious reactions taking the form of bed-wetting, fits of temper, and all the various personality difficulties. These are best met by carefully avoiding comparison of the eldest child with the second or neglecting him; he should be shown special marks of affection and enlisted as soon as possible as an assistant in the work of nursing and rearing the new arrival. The youngest of a number of brothers and sisters also may have special difficulties, to which particular attention should be given. Brotherly love is based on the love the parents feel and give to all alike, but it does not imply absolute equality. One experienced mother I knew used to cut the cake into unequal portions to make her children realize the inequalities of destiny.

Domestic servants should be treated as far as possible

as members of the family. The children should not regard them as mere servants but share the work with them as a matter of course. This will often play a real part in educating the servants too.

Marriage and Friendship

Marriage should not be an *égoïsme à deux* and so it normally includes friendships. They serve to give it living support and stimulus and can help decisively at critical moments. They are links with the great wide world of human society.

The ideal is friendship between married couples. This can be of inestimable value to the whole of their lives—and not only with people of their own age but with other generations too.

Besides this the wife will have her woman friends and the husband his man friends and a lot more "pals"—a word the wife will not quite understand at first. These more individual friendships are just as necessary but they should not take up time which ought to be devoted to the wife, nor should they be used to spite her. People who spend more than one or two evenings a week with friends not shared by their spouse are abdicating from married life. And people who complain about their wife or their husband to a "friend," or run down married life are helping to break up the marriage.

The most difficult thing is friendship between a married woman and a bachelor or a married man and an unmarried woman. Can such friendship exist? It can really only be called "pure friendship" if one realizes that there is always an erotic tension between a man and a woman and is always on one's guard against this and firmly resolved never to hide anything from the person to whom one is married. As long as the husband or wife can always share in the friendship and hear every word and see every movement and know the most secret feelings that are felt, the friendship will follow the right lines; but as soon as private meetings are felt to be necessary, as soon as the friend can no longer be spoken of freely and naturally, danger lies ahead and the thing must be squashed ruthlessly. "If your right eye causes you to sin, pluck it out," in fact. In times of doubt the following rule of thumb will be found extraordinarily useful: treat every woman as you would like any man to treat your wife.

Marriage and Work

Earning a living brings the family into contact with the outside world. Unfortunately in practice this job devolves mainly or entirely upon the husband and this easily creates tension or even rivalry between him and his wife; he thinks he is the only one who does any work or earns any money and she develops a defensive reaction against this, perhaps encouraging it however at the same time by undervaluing her household duties and envying him his work.

As against this it should be realized that in men's work a great deal depends on whether the man is married and if so what sort of wife he has. Married men are usually steadier, more conscientious and unruffled than bachelors, whilst bachelors often show more initiative and adaptability. An unhappily married man is sullen and irritable as a subordinate and domineering and moody in a position of authority. No words can express how much a good wife can do for her husband in the way of encouraging him in his difficulties, inspiring him in new ventures, and giving him fresh life and enthusiasm. This is true even though he may not notice it at the time, and only realize it afterwards in the pain of bereavement. It is also true that the husband's work is the business of both, even when it is too learned or technical for the wife to understand, for she always has some effect on her husband's personality—a dancer needs music, and no airman could get along without a ground staff. Work is to the husband what children are to the wife. The child belongs to the father as well as the mother but the latter is the "performing party" with a unique responsibility. In the same way the man acts as the "performing party" in his work, on their joint behalf. A wife must learn to accept the fact that her husband gives at least half his heart to his work. She would not be a good mother if she did not love her child as much as she does, and he would not be a good father if he did not love his job and want to do it well. The husband on his side must realize that, just as a marriage is damaged when a wife wants to be a mother to the exclusion of him, so it will be equally damaged by his being wrapped up in his work to the point of giving little or no attention to her. For many men their work and "spare time activities," societies and the like, simply mean a refusal to face their marriage problems. "It is more important to give time than money to one's wife," says Oeser.

When there are differences of opinion between husband and wife as to how much the husband ought to take on—should he accept this extra responsibility or extend his business, or start in a new field of work—then an attempt must be made to discover their separate motives. Is the husband obeying a sense of vocation, or a genuine professional or economic necessity, or is it a case of ambition, escapism, or a mere inability to say no? Is the wife objecting because of selfish possessiveness, or envy, or pettiness, or has she a better idea of his capacities and limitations and a better sense of what it is God's will for him to do? When work is thus understood as something in which husband and wife co-operate, it is clear that it is no solution for the wife to have outside work of her own. This may at times be an economic necessity; it may supply a psychological escape for a childless wife of a man engrossed in his work; but usually it is a flight from the family, a compensation for a feeling of inferiority, an unconscious form of revenge on the husband which boils down to, "I'm only paying you back in your own coin." Of course, the family income may go up as a result and the wife may feel better for it, but that does not make it any better really, any more than mutual consent makes adultery moral.

What both husband and wife usually underestimate is the value and importance of being a housewife. "The woman who succeeds in making her home a complete little world of its own has just as good a right to pride herself on it as the greatest statesman has on the way he rules his country." The atmosphere of a home is mainly determined by the wife and to a large extent the husband's success in his work depends on it, even more does the children's adjustment to life. A child that has enjoyed a harmonious peaceful home full of motherly love will never be defenseless in the face of evil; it has once and for all been given a sense of security. The American child psychologist Spitz says that in a certain district in Mexico where the mothers carry their children about for a year on their bare backs mental diseases seem to be quite unknown. He attributes this to the intimate contact between mother and child. A good home has exactly the same effect. Is any man's work of greater importance?

Keeping House Together

Being one flesh has a material application to finance and economics. This does not mean that "the husband earns the money and the wife spends it"; nor should it be continuously mentioned that it was the wife who brought the money into the family, even if she did. In marriage it is a case of each for all and all for each.

It is not true, despite what the self-appointed experts so often say, that most marriage problems are caused by money matters. But it is true that money problems are the field in which the struggle between opposing egoisms,

grievances, and unconscious longings for revenge can most
easily break out. If a husband is in the habit of doling out
the household expenses in small quantities, he is presuma-
bly compensating for a feeling of inferiority towards her
by making her feel his "power." (All dictators, in the family as in the world at large, are people with terrific inferiority complexes!) If the wife is always complaining to
her husband that he doesn't earn enough, unlike the man
next door, this very often signifies disappointment and even
hatred of him perhaps because she is unsatisfied erotically
or has not fully accepted her femininity.

The way people deal with economic matters is a general
index of more hidden elements in their character, and this
applies to married couples too. Anyone who has been in
the habit of spending all he gets becomes accustomed to
either living on credit or running into debt; and anyone
who in planning his budget always puts down all the favorable possibilities and makes no allowance for unforeseen
accidents will also get on badly when he marries and will
either come into conflict with his wife or else be reduced
to rags and his wife along with him. This is what makes the
installment plan so alluring to newly married couples who
want to buy furniture they cannot afford. But if misfortune
comes along and all the installments are not paid, all the
furniture, including the part already paid for, has to go
back; then the transaction usually takes on a moral aspect
and husband and wife level mutual accusations of thought-
lessness and pride at each other.

"Which of you, intending to build a tower, sitteth not
down first, and counteth the cost, whether he have sufficient to finish it?" For this reason engaged couples should
try to get an accurate idea of all the things they will need
when they are married.

Provision for a minimum material basis on which to
set up house is no mere middle-class prejudice but an essential contribution to a good start in marriage, for it

heightens the feeling of having a home. But if for any reason one is obliged to marry before the material basis is there, it is better to sleep on the bare floor and sit on old packing cases than to buy furniture on the installment system or go and live with in-laws. Newly married couples generally have a very inadequate idea of what their expenses will be since each is still thinking of what he or she has to pay as an individual. So an attempt must be made right away to get a bird's eye view of the whole business. The following are the most important items:—

Food 25–35%, or, in the case of small incomes, 40%, of the total income.

Rent 15%—in cities, alas, 25–30%, a most unfair burden on the budget as a whole.

Clothing (including cleaning) 6–10%

Insurance and taxes 8–15%

Heating and lighting 4%

Repairs and upkeep of house 2–4%

General, culture and education 5–8%

Pocket money (husband *and* wife) 5–10%

Unforeseen eventualities 10%

Gifts 5–10%

As will be seen, only minimum requirements have been taken into account. If more is spent on one item, economy must be exercised in another. "Savings" usually are put down as a separate item, but nowadays the money goes into life insurances or a pension fund. It is only reasonable also to have vacations and holidays, which in the sample above are supposed to be covered by "pocket money." The "Gifts" item—for the poor, or church, or welfare—should not be neglected for such offerings will bring a blessing on the whole house.

As to who pays for what, I adopt some suggestions from Hanni Zahner.

The income is divided (like Gaul) into three parts:

a) housekeeping money; i.e. food, gas, electricity, washing and cleaning materials, daily help, etc. This fund is dealt with by the wife.

b) money for rent, heating, taxes, insurance, subscriptions, papers, radio and TV, telephone. This is left to the husband.

c) money (what's left of it) for clothes, shoes, cultural items, presents, good causes, holidays, pocket money, dentist, etc. This is managed by both together, i.e. the expenditure is settled as each case arises.

Separate accounts are kept in all three cases.

As an alternative, the "docket" system may be adopted. "Permanent items of expenditure like rent, house maintenance, insurance, taxes, contributions, etc. are subtracted from the income and the remainder divided under various headings—'Clothes, shoes, washing'; 'Theatre, cinema, wireless, telephone'; 'Holidays, health, presents, good causes'; 'Pocket money and savings'; 'Unforeseen occurrences.'

"If the husband thinks the wife is using too much money for her housekeeping he should keep the accounts himself for a while and do the shopping, on Saturdays at least. That will probably soon teach him a lesson."

Keeping house together will teach husband and wife to think for and with each other as few other things can, and to be absolutely honest with each other. The wife who hides an item of expenditure from her husband, the husband who forgets to mention that he has had a raise, are beginning to be unfaithful to each other. "My money," "my requirements," "my obvious rights" are terms for which marriage has no room. We have to learn to say not "I," but "we." My cigarettes are no more important than my wife's scarf or perfume, and these are both far less important than an outfit for the coming child.

In marriage money can never be separated from mental

attitude: the items of expenditure are never "obvious" or conditioned by the "nature" of the thing we buy; they always express the feelings, the pattern of the inner life, the religious beliefs of the couple. A happy husband brings more home with him than a miserable one: a happy wife doesn't get tired easily. Many of the things on which husbands and wives spend money are in reality compensations for inward bitterness. Or they agree to give each other a treat of some sort for want of anything better to give. On the other hand, the bonds of a true family grow stronger for their being painfully short of material possessions.

What a family spends and saves is not determined by financial considerations but always in some way expresses their living spirit and helps to cement the love between them. So the parents economize on clothes or furniture so as to be able to take the children for a holiday—and thus gain quite a new fellowship with them. Or the husband will give up the idea of an attractive spare-time job so as to have the time for his wife and children. Husbands who without compelling necessity give up their whole time and energy to their business, ostensibly in order to "provide for the wife and children," are actually harming them by robbing them of a father. What benefit does a child get from having plenty of money in its "piggy-bank," or even from a better education, if it pays for it by never seeing its father in anything but a fuss. Money and education are things which can be picked up later on and are not guarantees of happiness anyway; whereas a child only has one father and is only young once.

But above all we show what we are made of by the way we give. The child who has been brought up to share with others, who has seen a cake or a bunch of flowers finding its way to a poor neighbor and something put aside for others even when it was hard to make ends meet, has learned something more important than anything on his school curriculum.

A simple workman has described how before he opens

his pay envelope he and his wife always kneel down in their kitchen and thank God for good health and work and wages. After that his pay always provides sufficient. But a man who deals with his household with a proper sense of responsibility, that is to say, regarding himself not as a "fortunate possessor" but as a steward whom God has put in charge of certain goods, will do his best also to see that his employees and fellow workers get a just wage—he will always remember "the righteousness of the kingdom of God" and enlist his whole family in its service.

"Give us this day our (not my) daily bread!"

6.

CRISES IN MARRIAGE

Marriage, being a "living and personal" affair, is bound to go through various crises, for crises mark development of every human organism. They are symptoms of the tension between one stage and the next, between our resistance to change and the need to alter our way of living. In marriage one person usually sees the need for this more clearly than the other and reproaches the other for holding back. Actually this gives a great opportunity for leading each other forward.

Growing Up

The first crises in marriage come from the simple fact of growing up together. Most people are not really adult when they marry, and they need to be helpful and patient with each other and prepared to give each other time.

Signs of a husband's failure to grow up are—continuing to be tied to his mother; being unable to make a real break with his parents' home; and being tied in an infantile fashion to his wife, treating her as if she were his mother. Having spoken of this in the first chapter, I need do no more than mention the matter here. Also there is the husband who refuses to assume the burden and dignity of leadership in the family. He dares not act as the proper "head" of the association—intending thereby, perhaps, to compliment his wife; but it must be said again and again that it is not only the husband's right but his duty to act as head, to assume responsibility, to make decisions, to take the initiative and figure as the final court of appeal in any disputes. Wives with any sense long for husbands who are this kind of leader and hate the idea of marriage as a two-headed or headless unit.

Only an immature wife objects to being "subordinate." She has still not grasped the profound polarity of the sexes, does not realize that she cannot be fully herself until she is the "heart" of the association, and that she can only be that when the man is its head. Here again no "rights" are involved; the question is whether husband and wife are playing the parts for which they were created in the beginning and which alone can make them happy. An abstract "feminism" remote from real life, the invention of sentimental men and masculine women, has confused people's ideas about this and done a great deal of harm.

Being grown up means accepting one's sexuality and the different sexuality of one's partner. Much has been written about the fundamental "conflict between the sexes" which exists within the animal kingdom outside the mating season. Enmity, contempt, or disgust may be observed among young boys before they start "growing up" and among girls till a still later stage. Chardonne says, "I believe that as a general rule youths resist love; not that they are modest or innocent, but they have an impulse to keep their freedom, a natural tendency to be as inaccessible as possible to love and the ways in which love expresses itself . . . love demands a kind of renunciation found only in mature men."

Inability to accept one's own or one's partner's sexuality is one of the most frequent causes of impotence and frigidity. One cannot teach young people too soon that their sexuality is natural and is complemented by the other sex. This is mainly the mother's job, during the first four or five years of a child's life. But most parents put a taboo on sex as something forbidden and indecent. No wonder their children take so long to grow up—and sometimes never do mature. Man, unlike animals, experiences the miracle of love, which is rooted in the difference of the sexes and builds on it the new unit, marriage.

Really adult human beings appreciate not only physical sexuality but also spiritual Eros and more than that—i.e. they can enjoy all their partner's physical and mental characteristics and control their own sexual powers and use them to make their partner happy. This too I have discussed at length already and we need not dwell on it here. The important thing at this stage is that the couple should not reproach each other for not being grown up but should help each other by striving to develop themselves.

Loving

A person may be quite grown up, and sexually mature, without knowing the meaning of love. In the early stages of marriage, people believe that love means the feeling of happiness they have in the presence of the other and vice versa. This seems to be so while they are in love with their own prefabricated picture of the person they have married, but this picture derives more from their imagination than from what that person really is. I have already referred to one aspect of this illusion, the anima projection. "Young people have an Idea of Love which does not conform to any human reality," says Chardonne. "One must learn to love a person throughout all the range of his being; this leads to a phase which causes a severe shock in all new marriages."

Once one has realized how very different one's wife or husband is from oneself and from the picture that exists in one's imagination, one begins to see how genuine love means the death of the ego:

*Hearts shudder before Love as though threatened by death;
For Love brings death to that dark despot, the self.*

These lines by the Persian mystic Jalal-uddin Rumi ought to bring encouragement to many a young married pair. After some experience of marriage one realizes that they are to be taken literally.

No one likes having to die and at first the self tries to dodge the issue. So there comes a phase in many marriages when each is to a certain extent trying to escape from the other. The husband decides that he must spend more time on his job, or at his club, or with his friends; the wife becomes more and more engrossed in her children, discovers other young wives similarly misunderstood by their husbands, and perhaps starts looking for "something to live for." Often this escape leads to some sort of excess—cigarettes, or drink, or gambling, morning coffee or confectionery, cinemas, or gossip. Sport, "improving oneself," and religion may become crazes in this sense, which means that they serve as impersonal material to fill an aching emptiness.

Of course this retreat is entirely unconscious. The couple feel disappointed in each other, or rather that they are not getting as much as they had hoped for out of their marriage. So they decide to look after number one, have a life of their own, and so regain their self-respect. This "life of one's own" is a depressive state which can take any form, from quiet resignation, through chronic bad temper, to constant misery. These are all ways of saying, "What an unfortunate mortal am I! And if nobody else notices it I must at least tell myself so." So one assumes tragic or heroic airs, and in both cases wallows in self-pity.

This is also a frequent cause of infidelity: either one tightens the bonds with parents, brothers, and sisters and goes through an infantile crisis or else takes up with some other person who will give understanding, sympathy, and affection. This is of course not for the sake of the person concerned but for the sake, again, of an imagined picture, so that the person may fulfill a function within our own selfish life. The boss is not really in love with his typist, but she inhabits a private world he has constructed to spite his wife.

If we ask for the meaning of this process, the only answer is that it is to avoid having to die. The paradox is that though in many marriages it seems to represent a definite break it is really an early stage, and an important manifestation, of true love. Through love the self must die, so it escapes into an egoistic world where there is no love. But love waits patiently for the self to resign itself to death.

True marriage begins when our self is prepared to die; when I am prepared to sacrifice my own will, my habits, my rights, my personal ambition, my private thoughts, my fantasies. These are real things—it may be reading in bed, week-end climbing, or a brilliant position in society. And it does not necessarily mean renouncing all these or yielding entirely to someone else's caprices but giving up deciding about them by myself, and taking somebody else's views into account. It is not a case any longer of "I" and "Thou," but of "us." (A still more important thing may be involved—my highest good, my religion or substitute for religion—they must be united in this matter above all things: this is an argument for the profound unsuitability of mixed marriages, unless the living Christ has freed the Roman Catholic wife and Protestant husband from their "religion" and, while fully preserving their membership of their separate Churches, has been so manifestly revealed within their life that they have together become a new creation.) In other words, marriage means the death of the self and rebirth to something new. If it is felt that such sacrifice or dying would be a betrayal of God, then the marriage should not be entered into. Indeed no one should ever enter into marriage with any reservations or any previous resolutions not to sacrifice certain things.

The marriage of two minds is symbolized in the biological procedure of conception: both maternal cell and paternal seed cell give up their individuality and die as such when they unite together. At that moment they start to develop and their existence begins to have a meaning. Married love is the greatest adventure imaginable: by it one human being is bound to another human being of whom he has only a subjective and maybe fragmentary notion and he gradually discovers the reality about this other being. One gives up one's own personality for this love not knowing where it will lead, for the other is at the same time losing his personality too. And from the two arises a new being of which neither had ever dreamed. This adventure is so overwhelming that it is ventured upon only by the unsuspicious or by people who cleave to God's word through all things and believe throughout the whole process that He stands firm and will not let them go. Anyone who builds on the foundation of his own personal feelings and sagacity will probably find that his house will not stand up against storms or floods or wind.

Married love has more to it than any other kind of love, however passionate. Basically it is something entirely different—a matter of life and death, dying and rising again, a state in which the self comes to an end and the child is born, where human love fails and is transfigured by the Love of God.

Fidelity

True and truly adult love between two human beings means fidelity. But such love is and always will be a gift; it does not depend on our own wills, and we cannot guarantee it. The one obligation to which we can bind ourselves by a free decision of the will is to fulfill the outward conditions in which love can grow and prosper, and these conditions may be described, approximately, as follows:

1) absolute honesty, or rather frankness towards the partner;

2) not to exchange any words, looks, or tokens of affection with any other person which we should not like our own husband or wife to see or indulge in themselves;

3) to seek the other's good in all circumstances, whether the other be friendly or hostile, healthy or sick, attractive or repulsive, faithful or unfaithful.

These three conditions give a concrete idea of what is meant by fidelity. If we beg afresh for God's love each day, then fidelity is the bowl we must hold out to Him for Him to put love into it. It is the one thing we can promise to do and keep to.

Nevertheless, most married people are tempted to be unfaithful at least once in the course of their married life —and of course they then feel that they are in an unusual or even unique situation which in some way justifies them in breaking one or more of the above conditions. As these "unique" situations occur every day I had better give a few examples, so that we may see how they work and be able to deal with them when they come along.

1. *"Bread and Cake."* Most people, men especially,

carry in their imaginations two opposing "ideal partners," for example a tall fair girl and a short dark girl. Experience shows that the type which provides the best wife is not always the type which exercises the most erotic attraction. When a man marries a wife of the "right" type and then meets the more "attractive" type, he easily imagines that he has made a mistake and missed his chance and must break up this mistaken marriage. One can only answer by saying that if you offer a child bread and cake it will always reach for the cake, but if you force the child to eat nothing but cake for a whole week it will be begging you to stop by the next evening, whereas it could go on eating bread for the rest of its life. A good wife is like bread, and one ought to thank heaven for her and not be led astray by any girl—even one as sweet as cake.

2. *Complementary Fulfillment*. People who suppress their urges and live in a somewhat forced and therefore not quite pure spirituality generally marry a partner with similar characteristics. They live by their joint religion, joint artistic or social or intellectual interests, and their erotic life takes a back seat. Then one of them may meet someone quite different, some simple fellow or frankly sensuous, primitive woman, who suddenly opens up the whole world that has been neglected and suppressed. Thus one finds highly intellectual and refined men suddenly falling in love with an incredibly primitive woman and projecting all the traditional womanly virtues on to her. The result is always catastrophic since the two are far too foreign to each other. Psychological consultation at such a time can often clarify and liberate what has been suppressed—and may often educate the other partner too—thus helping both to make a new beginning in which the neglected sides of their being will get a fresh chance.

3. *Heart and Head over Heels*. I have already mentioned that when the husband plays the "weak" and the

wife the "strong" role a very uncomfortable state of affairs arises. The husband hankers after a woman who will be weaker than he is himself and depend on him for assistance and look up to him; the wife hankers, if less consciously, for a strong man really superior to her who will guide and protect her and give her security. If one of them meets someone who seems capable of this part there is a temptation to infidelity. Frankness between husband and wife, and consultations with a neutral person who can see the false "head and heart" position between them, can help them not only to overcome a critical situation but to make their relationship permanently sound. This of course means that both have to undergo a basic inner transformation and die to their former habits and their own picture of themselves. It is one of the miracles of marriage that this should be possible.

4. *Banishment of Eroticism.* It is much more rare than is commonly believed for infidelity to take the form of an "irresistible," "once and for all" erotic harmony with a third person. The husbands of frigid wives and the still larger number of wives who without being frigid themselves are unable to get satisfaction from their husbands are exposed to a very strong temptation on meeting someone capable of supplying what they have so long lacked. They are inclined to project all the desirable characteristics onto this person and to subtract from the wife or husband the positive characteristics they actually possess. As a result they vastly overestimate the value of the erotic element and divorce it from its natural context. If in the meantime the marriage still holds together, it is looked upon as a "duty," an "imprisonment," because the erotic side of their marriage has been either undervalued or neglected altogether. If on the other hand the marriage is dissolved and the erotic "ideal" married, then catastrophe comes because a fairy prince loses his enchantment when one has to ask him for the household expenses or he finds the

soup too salty or grumbles over a badly ironed shirt, and the passionately beloved generally becomes a "stupid goose" or a "hysterical female" when it comes to setting up house or arranging the budget or even spending a fortnight's holiday with her. I do not mean by this to underestimate the power of passion or its pains but to issue a warning against isolating it from its proper context within love and marriage and banishing it from one's life. This latter course makes it practically impossible to enjoy or even see the more modest but very real erotic happiness that lies within marriage. A single infidelity, a single going "off the tracks," is often enough to upset the outlook of both partners entirely and to make it forever impossible to remedy what is still incomplete in the marriage. This will be clarified and expanded in the next two sections.

5. *Boredom and the Need for Variety.* Undoubtedly boredom is the most enslaving and also unfortunately the most widespread complaint in marriage. Generally it is not simply "fate" or "character" but the result of certain failings or rather sins which can be discarded, given a little dexterity and good will. I will enumerate a few:

(a) Lack of imagination or freedom in shaping one's life, so that one becomes an automaton. The husband leaves home every day at 7:30, returns at 12:15, lights his cigarette at 12:45, and at 2:30 rushes back to work. At 5:45 he listens to jazz or plays poker, supper is at 7, at 7:30 comes "the News"; every Wednesday, Thursday, and Friday there is a meeting of some society or other, on the other evenings he reads newspapers or works at his accounts until it is time for bed at 9:45 with "lights out" at 10:15. His wife has a weekly menu, so he can be certain, for instance, of getting beef and potatoes on Wednesday and cheese and coffee on Saturday. She has a weekday frock and a Sunday frock; the others hang in the wardrobe for "special occasions" and when they appear are thoroughly out of fashion. It is tacitly agreed that sexual intercourse shall take place every Wednesday and Saturday, but it doesn't last long.

(b) Lack of development of the personality, leading to enslavement by convention. The couple are resolutely determined to keep up with the Joneses and not to do anything that is not done. The wife may acquire a certain amount of culture and treat her husband to dissertations on diet, yoga, classical literature, and the theory of relativity; the husband expresses himself in strictly impersonal forms about the decadence of modern art and the bad manners of modern youth.

(c) Lack of frankness, so that either lies and secrecy create a reserve which makes real communion impossible or else feelings of guilt and inferiority choke all spontaneity and the pair have to stick to commonplaces. It needs maturity, trust, and genuine love for one to be absolutely honest with one's partner both about oneself and about her. It takes courage to be oneself and not to deck oneself out in borrowed plumes. Borrowed plumes are always boring in the long run anyway.

(d) Lack of tact as to when to keep quiet. Philosophic observations and short moral lectures delivered at the wrong moment are always irritating and boring, like telling the same story over and over again.

(e) Self-satisfaction, self-pity, self-righteousness, and self-absorption all make a person a bore. So do complaining, grumbling, moaning, moralizing, and always knowing better. A sense of humor is one of the most powerful antidotes against boredom and generally speaking one of the most important assets in marriage, so long as it does not express itself in gibes. No one without a sense of humor should ever get married.

Boredom comes from a lack of love. Love is time's living substance and time without love is a vast emptiness to be filled with rubbish—chatter, crossword puzzles, "fads," obsession with work, and above all philandering. Time which is not filled by love has to be "killed." There is no boredom in love, and when love has come to perfection it casts out boredom.

6. *Impersonal Sexuality*. Modern man tries to analyze everything into its constituent parts and then calls them the real thing. He isolates the chemical fragrance of a flower, investigates the constitution of hormones and vitamins—he even splits the atom, the symbol of indivisibility. In the same way he has isolated sex from love and then split sex into begetting and pleasure. And just as you can uncork a bottle and smell scent that has never been near a flower, so you can feel sexual pleasure that has no connection with love and will never produce a child.

The "progress" in all this is very questionable. Certain vitamins are less effective in their chemical purity than they are in their natural context in food and have to be reblended artificially. Highly concentrated perfume smells foul. And we know what happens when the atom gets split. The dangers of pleasure sought for its own sake are similar. Pleasure creates a bond of mutual dependence without there being any love to cement it and therefore it leads to misery and hatred: Don Juan is a misogynist and prostitutes despise the human male.

Pleasure sought for its own sake disturbs the harmony of marriage. It sets up standards by which the partner is compared with others and comes off worse: one woman has fuller breasts, another shapelier legs; this man has a more winning smile, that more self-confidence than my husband. Pleasure's only object is the satisfaction of desire, so when I am out to satisfy my desire I lust for my wife in the same way as I lust for any other woman, and I lust more for any other woman who promises to give me more pleasure than my wife. Insofar as this is so—and only if it is so—one may accept Tolstoy's paradox that the words, "He that looketh upon a woman to lust after her hath committed adultery with her," refer to lusting after one's own wife. It must of course be realized that what is evil is not the pleasure as such but the selfish search for pleasure for its own sake. To be "lustful" in this sense means to tear the pleasure out of the whole complex of love, to deprive love of its rightful pleasure. It is a fact that the man who lusts for his wife in this sense is continually plagued by lustful feelings for other women. Only when I love my wife honorably, love her as a person, do I develop the right attitude towards other women.

Now a good part of our so-called civilization consists in providing men with impersonal sexual pleasure to meet their lust. Books, magazines, and films supply them with hordes of seductive women; sex beckons them from every advertisement; they can hire women for as long as they like—and indeed most "respectable" women try to provoke men by artificially emphasizing some sexual attribute.

Leist speaks of the mania for nakedness which signifies a lack of pure love and affection. "Love is the way two human beings discover each other. As a result of this discovery they dare to transfer the ownership of themselves to each other and to regard and recognize each other as beloved husband and beloved wife. But this means that nakedness reveals the actual impenetrability of the mystery. In the unveiled 'Thou' we see the incomprehensible mystery of the person we love . . . Anyone who neglects this duty of meeting and this law of nakedness misses the very thing he is looking for in all his cravings. He is looking for mystery; but the looks that lust after nakedness seek this in vain and become ever more lustful and dissatisfied. Nakedness in which a mystery is unveiled occurs only within the sphere of Love; it is not a technique to be learned at will."

Is there any sense in swimming against the current and fighting against the waves of depersonalized sexuality? Prohibitions, denunciations, regulations enforcing decency may be necessary, like the police, but they can no more restore health to a country's love life than the police can create morality. Indeed, every list of prohibitions incites lust further: it is the greatest recommendation for a film to be "daring," "highly controversial," and "shortly due for censorship." But what we need to do is to disclaim all this mania for pleasure and show the significance of the pleasure and the senselessness of the mania.

If sexual pleasure is sought so strongly for its own sake and exalted so highly it is obviously because it is being neglected in marriage and regarded as inferior by what passes for Christian morality. We must start finding our pleasure in our marriages! Everyday experience shows that pleasure outside marriage is short lived and leaves a sense of dust and ashes. "Love is much more than love," says Chardonne; it always points away from itself and is only happy when it is taken up into some greater context. The problem is not how to fight impersonal isolated sexuality grown rank but how to give marriage once again, or perhaps for the first time, its fullness, its riches, its pleasure, its blessings.

7. *True Love outside Marriage.* It may happen, though much more rarely than is usually imagined, that love for a third person becomes a revelation of genuine true love and a marriage already contracted is seen to have been an error, perhaps the result of egoistic or solely erotic motives. This gives rise to genuine tragedies like the story of Tristan and Isolde, *La Nouvelle Heloïse,* Fogazzaro's *Daniele Cortis.* The purer this love is the more rarely does it lead to physical adultery: Tristan lays his sword of chastity between himself and Isolde. Occasionally a divorce leads to a new and happy marriage, but this does not necessarily justify it. Much oftener divorce leads people to realize that the second affair was not as extraordinary as they imagined and that the mediocrity of their first marriage was their own fault. So if a husband or a wife are tempted, they should not immediately see themselves as Tristan and Isolde but fight against the temptation and regard it as a sign of immaturity and lack of love. And if

the "other love" does happen to prove great and sacred, then let their marriage nevertheless remain marriage and let their love purify the lovers in the fire of suffering. If Tristan and Isolde had given way, if Isolde had immediately got a divorce from King Mark, then no one would have had anything further to say about them—they would have fallen into oblivion, like all the other adulterers, great and small.

To be faithful in such circumstances often entails a heroic struggle. It means not only a battle against external temptation or immaturity in oneself or one's partner but a struggle for a more complete marriage, a richer life, for God's effective and visible blessing. The tempted husband or wife wrestles with God like Jacob and says, "I will not let thee go except thou bless me."

Fidelity entails a real struggle when it is the other party who has been unfaithful. It should be remembered that usually both parties have a share in the guilt of adultery, and the one who is innocent in the eyes of the law should take the first step by confessing his own guilt and asking for forgiveness. This will make it easier for the other to admit his guilt and regret it.

Fidelity then means rebuilding the marriage with new love, faith, and courage.

Change

Young married people tremble a little at the thought of the years that lie ahead, when life's joys will have ended and their way be all downhill. And people in their forties, who are generally disappointed with their lives so far, are notoriously keen to get in one last fling—feeling that during the next few years they must somehow fulfill their great ambition and have one grand affair and get a little real happiness at least. The husbands, despite decreasing strength, work harder and harder and collapse after ten years with high blood pressure or heart trouble; the wives make a desperate effort to look younger with the help of cosmetics or keep-fit movements; and both are tempted to give proof of their virility or powers of attraction by forming some extramarital liaison. There are very few men who have not experienced this temptation at some time between the ages of forty and sixty, and those who have given in to it know the misery it brings. Such an attitude is the result of having failed to realize what fullness of life is. Western man, unlike for instance the Chinese, regards twenty-five years old as the ideal age: strength, passion, virility, fitness, good looks, ease of manner—these are absolute values and all men are measured by them. In consequence it is taken for granted that degeneration sets in at thirty and that at fifty a man is finished. But life possesses other values—gentleness, integrity, peaceableness, patience, friendliness, kindness, stability, understanding, reliability, wisdom, maturity, humility. These qualities increase with age and at fifty a man is just beginning to realize that they can exist.

It is just as silly to set up an eighteen-year-old girl as the ideal of womanly beauty. A fifty- or sixty-year-old woman possesses qualities infinitely more attractive to a mature man. He may be more excited by a young woman, but is he simply a mechanical device whose parts are body and sex? Has he no need for fellowship, affection, understanding—fellowship far beyond the horizon of a woman many years younger than himself? And even though a young woman may at first get a certain thrill from the attentions of a mature and experienced man, she would have strong misgivings if she felt that he was only interested in her body. Anyone seriously tempted to get a divorce at fifty or sixty and "begin life all over again" with a young woman should consider this: That if a sixty-year-old man has a splendid old lime tree standing in his garden and suddenly decides that a nut tree would look better he can if he likes cut down the old tree and plant the young one in its place, but he will not be able to sit in the shade of it for a long time—until he is lying under it, in fact, in his grave.

A married couple therefore should aim at maturity, help each other and their union to mature, and after fifty years together they will not only be as happy as they were on their wedding day but their love will be incomparably richer and deeper and more satisfying. A marriage which suffers shipwreck during the years of change does so because it has the wrong cargo on board and has obtained its only nourishment from the necessarily ever diminishing physical element. In a really living marriage decreasing vitality and the arrival of wrinkles are hardly noticed at all, for Eros more than makes up for the former and the wrinkles only deepen the expression of features loved more and more with every day. What has been said about the "mastery" of sex is peculiarly applicable to a marriage as it grows older. Renunciation of something which one is still capable of having is fruitful and freedom-giving. At this point a new voyage of discovery begins within love, and only the genuinely mature are equipped for it.

No one who is granted the grace of a long marriage need fear the "critical years." They follow as harvest time follows summer bloom. Together two can learn the sublime art of growing old, which in its turn will lead them, all illusion gone, to the gates of eternity.

Divorce?

But are there crises which kill marriage, and must divorce be permitted when a marriage is dead? This is the old, old question.

Jesus has given his answer: "What God hath joined together, let not man put asunder."[1] For a marriage which

1 Mark 10:9.

really is a marriage there can be no grounds whatsoever
for divorce. There is nothing shaky or doubtful about this:
marriage can no more be dissolved than a living body can
be cut in two even when the civil law recognizes grounds
for divorce and a court makes out the decree, husband
and wife—not to speak of the children—carry their broken
marriage with them as long as they live. Every divorcee
knows all too well the truth of this. The gospels take a
more realistic view of marriage than the civil law. To ensure this truth, the Roman Catholic Church requires people to renounce the right to civil divorce, and we must be
grateful for this.

But are there no exceptions? Did not Jesus himself[2] recognize adultery as giving grounds for divorce? It should
be noticed in this connection that the original text refers
to "porneia," which means whoredom, not adultery; and in
any case this proviso is not to be found in the gospels of
Mark or Luke or in the First Epistle to the Corinthians,
so there is a chance that it may be a later insertion. All
the same there are indeed marriages which are no marriages at all because the elementary conditions of marriage
have never been taken seriously by either of the partners.
As Karl Barth says, "It is an outmoded heresy that marriage is simply a wedding service, and vice versa. Two
persons may be married and yet never live together in a
marriage worthy of the name." In this case it is not a matter
of dissolving a marriage but of declaring the annulment of
a relationship which never was a marriage at all. This is
the point of view taken quite consistently by the Roman
Catholic Church, the Church of England, and the Greek
Orthodox Church. In the latter two a bishop decides
whether a marriage should or should not be declared null;
in the Roman Catholic Church the conditions of annulment are clearly laid down by canon law.

In this matter the Protestant Churches have often been

[2] Matt. 5:32; 19:9.

too lax in recognizing the remarriage of divorced persons in church. The practice in some parts of studying the civil documents and deciding each case on its own merits is all right in theory but does not seem to work out very well in practice. In Germany the United Lutheran Churches have recently declared the remarriage of divorced persons to be as a rule invalid.

More important than this seem to be the grounds on which the justification for the remarriage of divorced persons is based. It is not that any "causes" are admitted as directly justifying divorce, for the Protestant Churches too regard divorce as "a sign of our failure to keep to the order set forth in the Gospel," and understand it as existing "because of the hardness of our hearts": it is not a matter of "permission" but forgiveness. If these Churches do recognize the remarriage of divorced persons they do so not in the name of any right or law but solely in the name of Christian forgiveness, which can even wash away the sin of divorce. It thus becomes clear that this view presupposes an inner revolution, a repentance (*metanoia*), which is totally lacking in a great many cases of remarriage. Where this lack is obvious—and expressions of regret have necessarily to be taken at their face value—the Church should refuse to remarry.

The Catholic and Protestant attitudes to divorce therefore do not differ fundamentally. Both deny the existence of any legal right to divorce and recognize at most the annulment of a proceeding that has only been a marriage in appearance. But while the Roman Catholic Church holds inexorably to its fundamental principle, lest by showing indulgence in any cases whatsoever it should be helping to spread the disease of divorce, the Protestant Church asserts that Christian living is based entirely on forgiveness and that this truth must be applicable even in the matter of divorce.

What attitude should a practicing marriage counselor adopt in this matter? The Christian principle of the indissolubility of marriage must be his basis, but he will come across many relationships which have none of the essential attributes of true marriage and others which were perhaps once marriages but now resemble decaying corpses. Like a physician working on an apparently lifeless body he will use all his resources to restore such marriages to life, and experience will teach him to display more courage and patience than do the husband and wife themselves. He will point out to them that marriages contracted under false assumptions have often come to life as time went on and even become very happy ones, and he will try to get them to see the grave consequences of divorce. Finally, if he is himself a believer, he will hint at the possibility of a miraculous change through a profound inner readjustment. But it is not for him to pass judgment, or to deny the help divorce may give in situations which, humanly speaking, have no other way out. A marriage in ruins may be saved by the grace of God but not by mere will power or a hard and fast rule. The true doctor learns humility. So does the marriage doctor.

Remarriage

What is to happen when one of the married pair dies? Oeser says, "There are marriages which come to an end with the death of one of the parties. There are others which really deserve the name of marriage." But a real marriage will not come to an end with a second marriage but accompany the survivor first through his great sorrow and then in his new journey to further development.

In practice, the earlier the age at which widowhood starts, the more clearly, usually, a second marriage is indicated, especially when there are young children, whereas after a long and happy marriage remarriage generally brings disappointment. In any case a second marriage should always be based on genuine inclination just as much as the first and not simply because of loneliness and a need to fill the gap: only then can both marriages fulfill their whole meaning. Second marriages should be regarded as a serious undertaking; they often prove a very hard one indeed.

A widow who has been happily married suffers severely. At first she feels as if half her body had been amputated. To whom will she go with all the feelings and experiences that fill her mind? Who is there to hold her by the hand when some difficult step has to be taken? Who will give her security? Often after a short time friends gradually begin to shun her as if they were afraid of her. She experiences the depths of loneliness: widowhood is a humiliating state. But at this very point she can begin to learn that God is the special patron and protector of widows and that He can make her heart sing for joy. A sense of the blessing of her marriage floods her whole being and gently spreads love, joy, and peace around her.

Marriage Counseling

To end this chapter on marriage crises I must try to indicate briefly what external assistance is available toward avoiding them or resolving them once they have arisen.

The science of marriage is a young science, in fact it is still only rudimentary. Practically it covers three different fields.

1) Introducing children to the problem of sex. The chief requirement here is that the parents have or gain a proper attitude themselves, for it is they, especially the mother, who must acquaint their children with these problems in the individual way nature demands. In general, it should be borne in mind that all questions as to where babies come from, how boys differ from girls, what part the father plays in begetting children, etc., should always be answered

absolutely truthfully even when they are put by two- or three-year-olds. At eight the child should be fully acquainted with the biological side of human sexuality. During adolescence he should be told or read about the significance of the sexual feelings now awakening in him.

2) Direct preparation of young people for marriage and choice of partner. This may be done through lectures and discussion groups, instruction courses for engaged persons, books or letters of instruction, and finally by means of personal talks with a parson, doctor, or marriage counselor. Similar courses also may be held for young married persons.

3) The treatment of conflicts and other problems in marriage. This extends from simple psychological explanations or budgeting advice to treatment of sexual disturbances which can lead to the final break of adultery or the chronic ruin of a marriage. Here the marriage counselor can work in collaboration with divorce court judges.

Marriage counsel centers are being set up in an increasing number of cities; they are well used and do excellent work. In England, non-professional people are being trained for this work and take it on as an honorary or spare-time job. However, it is desirable that all spiritual directors and practicing doctors should receive training in the science of marriage, since it is one of the main causes of psychological illness—not only among married people, but especially amongst their children—and this precise point offers the widest opening to spiritual direction.

In Switzerland, Christian interdenominational training courses for professional or spare-time marriage counselors are being organized, and these courses also include practical work in some marriage counsel center. The object of marriage counseling is not to prevent a few divorces but to increase the number of happy marriages and to win for the married state an entirely new esteem. Therefore, it cannot be based only on biological or psychological knowledge or on a few technical tricks found useful in the past but has to be based on a comprehensive view of marriage as an integral part of the whole order of human existence.

It is up to the modern marriage counselors to develop an independent "Science of Marriage" not limited to the study of sexuality or fertility or morals, but concerned with marriage as a living entity.

7.

THE MYSTERY OF MARRIAGE

The lowest organisms increase by simple subdivision; the same living substance goes on prolonging itself endlessly and hopelessly. At a later stage male and female seminal cells blend to form a new organism: the single individual has no function except to carry the seminal cell and so propagate the species; it is merely a "temporary appendage to the seed plasma." At a still later stage animals are sexually differentiated and gradually become independent individuals: the male develops aggressive and food-providing attributes; the female, having to care for her young, becomes the protective element, and generally speaking the more of a mammal she is the more something resembling a personal relationship appears between mother and child. At this stage a personal relationship also develops between male and female, who not only meet in the brief period of fertilization, after which the female may in some cases devour the male as soon as his work is done, but live together during the period when the young require care, and often permanently, sharing the work between them and looking after each other. Here one can see the beginnings of marriage.

And then, in human marriage, another cycle of evolution occurs, from functionalism to personal freedom. Primitive marriage is mainly an association for maintaining life and begetting children. Even when the men, whose biological function leaves them more spare time, develop art and technology and create a whole culture, this has very little immediate effect on their married life. In Greek civilization, for example, married women were mainly house-keepers and child rearers and their husbands went off to the *hetaira* for intellectual companionship. During the Christian era married women acquired a new dignity and were—very nearly—accepted as real persons; but, as the art of love grew more and more ethereal and refined, it did not have the wife as its object but some ladylove who might be on the spot or up in some remote tower. *Tristan und Isolde*, the *Vita Nuova*, *La Nouvelle Heloïse*, *Die Wahlver-wandtschaften*, *Anna Karenina* and most of the other great romances dismiss marriage as a second-rate, smug, domes-tic form of love. So La Rochefoucauld could say, "Il y a de bons mariages, mais il n'y en a point de delicieux," while Kant produced the appalling statement that marriage is "the union of two persons of opposite sex with a view to the lifelong possession of each other's sexual parts."

Paradoxically it needed the two roundabout routes of anti-marriage love poetry on the one hand and the equally anti-marital feminist movement on the other to bring men and women to the realization that even marriage could, and should, be a perfect love relationship. And—paradox-ically again—marriage began to be criticized as an institu-tion and divorces began to pile up because people were beginning to feel that marriage did not always realize this. People had gone on for thousands of years without coming up against this problem because no one had ever thought of expecting such a miracle from marriage.

So today, for what may well be the first time in history, we find ourselves in a situation in which husband and wife expect to derive love's highest happiness from marriage but have no clear idea as to how this is to be effected. In the past, literature has either portrayed the ideals of love in a non-marital setting—where reality did not have to be faced (. . . and they lived happily ever after) or it admitted to a very solid ideal for marriage but one in which love plays a very subordinate part indeed. Today there are occasional married couples who prove that the full happiness of love is possible—and only in marriage—and that marriage can be a really living thing—but only through love. And again it is gradually being realized that this union of love and marriage is possible only through an exceptional grace from God—the blessing He explicitly promises to marriage. Is this really such a new discovery? In theory, perhaps not. But I do not believe that cause and effect have ever before been followed to the very end with such consistency and conscientiousness—the biological basis of marriage, its sociological significance, the psychological relationship between husband and wife on the one hand and parents and children on the other, and along with all this the theological view of marriage with husband and wife one flesh in the eyes of God. Not until one sees all this as an integral whole can one realize the fact and at the same time the mystery of marriage.

Change

A husband and wife who live together in true marriage are changed in the depths of their being. This is not only because they suit each other as lovers or because they have formed a genuine "I and Thou" relationship but because in their marriage a mysterious power is at work, like the organic power to assimilate nourishment and change it into living substance. "Reciprocal inward development and a continuous endeavor to lead each other to perfect fulfillment" is the external aspect of this mystery, but at bottom it is a supernatural transformation, for they lead each other far further than they have reached on their own or can anticipate.

However, there are happy marriages in which the two think only of each other's happiness, love each other quite selflessly, and in fact idolize each other. Such marriages lead away from God, since the two are dearer to each other than God. This must in the end be fraught with evil consequences for both; true love cannot wish to separate anyone from God. It is thus a sign of real marriage not to idolize each other, not to live entirely for each other and be utterly dependent on each other, but to recognize all love and pleasure as coming from God, loving wife or husband as their mediator rather than their source. Eros is then no longer a natural primitive force by which one human being subjugates and dominates another, but a fragment of divine love made flesh through which married people bless and liberate each other.

If success is attained within marriage in giving and receiving love in this way, then husband and wife minister to each other and their marriage is a permanent means of sanctification for them both. This not only exercises its influence on the sexual side of their relationship but brings about a gradual transformation of their whole lives, as persons, as a family, and as members of a church. When a couple share in a real marriage this necessarily affects others: the two are no longer living for themselves but feel themselves to be members of an order which includes other members of equal value with themselves with Christ as its head. Their thoughts and looks are pure, for they keep their impulses in their proper place and seek no mysteries except where they properly belong, i.e. within marriage. They let the love that God has bestowed upon them go out to other human beings. They are orderly and conscientious about material things, knowing that everything in their home has spiritual significance and that in a life which is genuinely alive nothing can be either dead or without its influence.

But then are we to take it that this grace exists only for the married, and that the unmarried are to be relegated to an inferior status? The fact is that marriage involves not merely human love and happiness but a gift and a grace and, paradoxical as it may seem, it is for this very reason that the unmarried are able to share in it. It is therefore up to men and women, particularly women, not to grab at love whenever it offers itself in either a sentimental or grossly physical form but to accept their destiny as coming from God Himself, whether it brings them marriage or celibacy.

The notorious "bachelors" or "old maids" are people who have not accepted their destiny, whether in marriage or in celibacy. There are just as many married "bachelors" and "old maids," in this sense, as unmarried men and women who draw from God's grace.

Over marriage stands the text, "Behold, I make all things new." All things can really become *new*. However dubious the situation may look, however little is to be expected of the future—all things can become new.

All things therefore must become new. A partial revision is no use. A man cannot make a new beginning in the erotic sphere and go on managing his income egoistically or imposing upon other people. In a complete union for life everything must be thrown into the melting pot.

But it is the second word which is most important: the *I* who makes all things new. This is not achieved by our own talents or efforts; it is Christ who creates us anew. Insofar as we are united to Him we are always as if we were at the beginning of creation. Heredity and psychological complexes, wrong choices and erotic failure, even death and sin, no longer have any power over us, since He really has risen from the dead, and He makes all things new.

Is Marriage a Sacrament?

I have said earlier that the individual human being is one-dimensional, like a line standing on its own in space. Marriage, on the other hand, is two-dimensional; it forms a plane on which something can rest. Now it is obvious that two symmetrical figures like right and left hands can never be made to coincide, however much they are moved about on the same plane. Only when they are transferred to the third dimension, that of space, can they be made to coincide. God forms the third dimension in marriage. He makes the space and depth in which miracles happen and things coincide in a way impossible on the purely human plane. When it is not only husband and wife who say Yes to each other, but God too says His great Yes to their marriage, then within their marriage things become possible which would be impossible outside it. God's Yes applies even if the marriage is not a happy one from the human point of view, even if the choice has been an unsuitable one, even if sickness or other adversity makes harmony difficult to achieve. God's Yes is independent of these human considerations; it is objective and self-subsisting, and if one holds firmly by it, it works miracles. When Luther was tempted by the devil he wrote on a piece of paper the words *"Baptizatus sum"* ("I am baptized"), clinging to God's promise. When we are tempted we too can say, "I am married," and God will make His promises for our marriage effective. If I understand it aright it is this objective blessing of God's, this effectiveness of the divine promise independent of all psychological laws and human willing, which the Roman Catholic Church calls a sacrament. We need not quarrel as to whether this mystery is of equal dignity with baptism and the Lord's Supper; the main thing is to recognize the fact of it, no matter what name we call it by. But it is just this very fact of the supernatural blessing that rests upon marriage that we have to a very great extent lost all power to understand. For far too long we have regarded marriage as a purely biological business hedged round by rigid moral laws. Marriage has consequently fallen a victim to the biologists, and suffered a worse fate still by falling into the hands of the moralists. It is high time for Protestant circles to return to a theological conception of marriage.

"When the Perfect Comes"

The ultimate meaning of marriage is not contained in marriage, nor is it to be found in the children; it consists in the "reciprocal inner development of two married persons" with the object of making each other obedient to God, or rather of doing God's will together. For the married, God's love at first expresses itself in married human love, not only as Agape but also as Sex and Eros: "Corporeity is the end of God's way," Oetinger has written. Yet this form of love, when clearly understood, leads truly married people away from themselves and towards God.

Marriage is a path to be traveled together, and the "marriage house," with its hearth, is only a resting place on the way. I may scandalize the romantic feelings of honeymoon couples when I say that marriage does not last forever, for "In the resurrection they neither marry, nor are given in marriage."[1] However, if there is to be a resurrection of the person, there also will be a resurrection of "that person, marriage." It may well be very different from marriage as we know it now. It will be free from selfish lust and possessiveness, dogmatizing and moralizing. In marriage we seek God together; in the resurrection we shall be rec-

[1] Matt. 22:30.

ognized by Him together, and the whole weight of the earthly bond, all the nostalgic wistfulness and loneliness of life on earth and the pains of earthly love will drop away from us. "Love never ends . . . but when the perfect comes, the imperfect will pass away."[2]

[2] I Cor. 13:8, 10.

INDEX